TEXAS

PUBLIC

GARDENS

TEXASPUBLICGARDENS

ELVIN McDONALD

PHOTOGRAPHY BY

KEVIN VANDIVIER

EARL NOTTINGHAM

PELICAN PUBLISHING COMPANY
Gretna 2008

This is a Pinafore Press book
Concept and design by Janice Shay
Production assistance by Angela Rojas
Editing by Betsey Brairton, Nina Kooij
Index by Sara Levere

Photography by Kevin Vandiver: pp. 9, 11-19, 37-39, 41-45, 47-51, 53-57, 59-63, 69-71, 77-81, 83-87, 95-99,
113-115, 117-118, 119, 121-125, 139-143, 151-153, 155-159, 167-169, 171-173, 181-183, 185-189
Photography by Earl Nottingham: pp. 5, 6, 21-29, 31-35, 65-67, 73-75, 89-93, 101-106, 109-111, 127-131,
134, 136-137, 145-149, 161-165, 175-179
Portrait of Lady Bird Johnson and Laura Bush by Kevin Stillman/*Texas Highways Magazine*: p. 119
Additional photography by Randy Mallory: pp. 133, 135

ISBN-13: 9781589805675

Cover photography by Kevin Vandivier and Earl Nottingham
Portrait of Elvin McDonald by Ted Betz

Printed in China

Published by Pelican Publishing Company, Inc.
1000 Burmaster Street, Gretna, Louisiana 70053

DEDICATION

*Mary M. Wilson, a constant friend since we
worked together at Buell Greenhouses
in Eastford, Connecticut, the spring of 1956*

John W. Zickefoose, my life partner since New Year's Eve, 2001

*And a 10-gallon hatful of thanks to
Janice Shay, Earl Nottingham and Kevin Vandivier*

CONTENTS

I have been a fan of public gardens since visiting my first as a 17-year-old—the Missouri Botanical Garden in St. Louis. Writing this book has been exciting work for me, largely because Texas quite possibly has more remarkable public gardens than any other state. The small Panhandle town of Perryton, where I attended grade school, has always prided itself on making the public park as green as possible, with tubs of petunias and geraniums and plenty of locally adapted Chinese elms to shade the picnic tables.

In 1992, soon after I moved to Houston from New York City, I was invited to participate in a charrette at the Garden Center to hear Laurie Olin's plans for renewing and improving Hermann Park. Philadelphia-based Olin is respected internationally. Olin was brought in to renew what had been Houston's "lungs" for nearly a century. His "The Heart of the Park at Hermann Park" earned him the American Society of Landscape Architects Award of Excellence in 2005.

Three characteristics about the work on Hermann Park are held in common by most of the gardens in this book: 1) The gestation period for a great garden, arboretum or park—from identifying the need, hiring a designer, agreeing on the design, raising the funds, construction and planting—is typically measured in decades rather than years. 2) It is important to hire the most talented design help you can afford, and if he or she should happen not to be all that familiar with locally adapted and native plants, help them enlist the best horticulturist in town. 3) Public gardens grow and change in time and space, like no other art form. Re-thinking and updating them is inevitable.

When planning this book I looked for outstanding public gardens in every part of the state, because I know that Texans all over the state—north, south, east and west—have always (literally) put down roots, dreaming of creating an oasis.

During the years I lived in Houston, I traveled widely, giving talks and taking pictures. Texas gardeners are savvy about what will grow in their climate, which can vary from USDA Zone 6a (to -10 degrees F) in the north of the state to 9b in the south (occasional frosts), with annual rainfall anywhere from 8 to 48 inches. And sizzling summers for all. Living in Houston, I learned there were five seasons—fall, winter, spring, summer, and Hell.

Besides geographic considerations in selecting the gardens, I also looked for differences. The Bell Park Cacti Garden in Hale Center is as different from the Cullen Sculpture Garden at the Museum of Fine Arts in Houston as Mars is from Venus. And I discovered many similarities: The Tyler Rose Garden and the Fall Festival in October are, in my opinion, second only to the Pasadena Rose Parade. The Dallas Arboretum has almost as many tulips as Holland, and its topiaries set the standard for the new age of an old garden art form.

Miss Ima Hogg's Bayou Bend gardens in Houston is the quintessential place to see azaleas and magnolias in bloom. And up the road at Nacogdoches there's the Stephen F. Mast Arboretum with more than 850 different azaleas. There are several authentic Japanese gardens within the pages of this book and the Forbidden Gardens in Katy are a glimpse into ancient China.

When I lived in Houston I learned to embrace that fifth season by celebrating the plants that grow spectacularly in the heat. Ornamental gingers, Chinese hibiscus, canna lilies, elephant-ears, caladiums, passion flowers, jasmines, bougainvillaea, okra (because it's my favorite vegetable), orchids and bromeliads. When I moved to Des Moines in 1995, I learned that Iowa also has the fifth season; not as protracted, but just long enough to bring in the corn, a tropical grass.

We visit public gardens for many reasons. They are places to be alone with our thoughts or to be happy with a crowd, for a wedding, anniversary, family outing or picnic. I look for new plants and better ways to grow what I have. On a visit to the Mercer Arboretum I met up with sun-tolerant 'Alabama Sunset' coleus, which makes a glowing brick-red-chartreuse shrub in one season—either in Humble or in Des Moines. I believe we never outgrow the human need to interact with nature. No matter how we hurtle through cyberspace, it still takes nine months to have a baby and a radish can't be hurried through a fax machine.

—*Elvin McDonald*

Note to garden visitors: Because visiting hours and phone numbers change, I have not listed them in the garden descriptions. Each garden in the book has a website (see page 192) for up-to-date information.

AMARILLO BOTANICAL GARDENS

Founded as the Garden Center in 1958, these four green acres in the Medical Center Park of Amarillo have recently benefited from a multimillion dollar facelift. As a relatively young institution, the Center has been able to move quickly in creating regionally relevant gardens representing the diversity of plants that gardeners in the Texas Panhandle may use in ecologically friendly landscaping.

The Yellow Garden in the entry celebrates Amarillo and the Golden Spread region itself. Native and adaptive plants featuring the color yellow occupy an island bed in a surround of desert willows, *Salvia greggii*, catmints and Russian sage arranged among red boulders and accent rocks. The nearby Fragrance Garden abounds with spring bulbs, lilacs, mock oranges, roses and viburnums. There are also lavenders and mints, rosemarys and thymes.

Across the path is the Butterfly Garden, which incorporates all that butterflies need: nectar plants, larval or host plants, water and mud seeps, basking rocks and habitat choices. In order to be ecologically friendly, the policy is to rarely, if ever, use herbicides or pesticides. The cistern bordering the garden demonstrates a sound water conservation technique.

The path next leads to a shaded lawn area with arbors and benches so that guests may pause to take in the Shade Garden with its many flowering shrubs and woodland foliage plants, and the Wedding Garden. Adjacent is the Four Seasons of Color Garden, sited to surprise visitors with new vistas at every turn. The Sculpture Garden recognizes Southwestern heritage—wind, the prairie, the rocks and plants of Palo Duro Canyon 27 miles southeast of the city.

Not many steps away is the Wagner Japanese Garden, with the essential elements of water, rock, form and structure as a setting for various foliages and textures. Lanterns, pagodas, bamboo and a bridge complete the expression of an Eastern-style landscape.

The jewel in that crown of the Amarillo Botanical Gardens is the Mary E. Bivins Tropical Conservatory, named for the late philanthropist, a woman who was passionate about her own gardens. The Conservatory qualifies as a "green building," which is to say it is a self-contained system that uses minimal energy. Besides the fascinating collection of rain-forest plants, it is home to Stan the tree frog and local celebrity Cracker, a young Military Macaw.

Offices, meeting rooms and a 1,600-volume library are housed in the main building. Educational programs target all populations. Of particular note is the comprehensive horticulture curriculum designed for health care workers who wish to practice horticultural therapy.

INSIDE THE MARY E. BIVINS TROPICAL CONSERVATORY, VISITORS KNOW INSTANTLY THEY HAVE STEPPED INTO ANOTHER WORLD—ONE QUITE DIFFERENT FROM THAT OUTDOORS, WHERE DRYING WINDS AND TEMPERATURE EXTREMES GO WITH THE TERRITORY. A WATERFALL AND POND WITH GOLDFISH ARE SURROUNDED BY LUSH AND EXOTIC FOLIAGE FROM RAIN-FOREST PLANTS USED FOR FOOD, MEDICINE, CLOTHING OR HABITAT.

ACREAGE: 4 ACRES

SEASONAL BLOOMS: GARDENS AND CONSERVATORY ASSURE ALL-SEASON INTEREST

OTHER ATTRACTIONS: SPACE RENTALS FOR SPECIAL OCCASIONS; SITED AT THE MEDICAL CENTER

The Friends Plaza makes a dramatic entrance to the Mary E. Bivins Tropical Conservatory. On nice days—and there are more of them than the region gets credit for—this is a popular gathering spot for employees and visitors from the neighboring Medical Center.

BANANAS AND OTHER TROPICAL
FRUITS THRIVE IN THE
CONSERVATORY, ALONG WITH
ORCHIDS, BROMELIADS AND OTHER
RAIN-FOREST NATIVES—MANY OF
THEM FAMILIAR AS HOUSEPLANTS.
SET FREE FROM THEIR POTS,
SILVERY CHINESE EVERGREENS,
PEACE LILIES AND ANGEL-WING
BEGONIAS GROW WITH ABANDON.

Valentine anthuriums (above), which also come in white and pink, bloom almost constantly in the Conservatory.

The flamboyant flowers of Chinese hibiscus (above right) last just a day or two at most, but they appear year-round on new growth.

THE THORNY KAPOK (ABOVE LEFT)
IS NOT A TREE TO HUG. IN ITS
NATIVE TROPICAL AMERICA, AFRICA
AND EAST INDIES, THE THORNS
DETER FORAGING ANIMALS.
DUTCH IRIS (ABOVE) WELCOME
SPRING IN THE OUTDOOR GARDENS,
ALONG WITH CROCUS, HYACINTHS,
TULIPS AND DAFFODILS.

ANTIQUE ROSE EMPORIUM

G. Michael Shoup, owner of the Antique Rose Emporium, fell in love with his first rose in 1982 and, like that proverbial first potato chip, he just couldn't stop. Today his nursery cultivates more than 300 old roses, numerous of them dating to the early 19th century, notably Champneys' 'Pink Cluster' (1811), the Chestnut rose (a species known prior to 1814), 'Blush Noisette' (1817) and 'Felicite Parmentier' (1834).

As Mike tells the story, it was 'Mermaid' that opened his eyes. "I was in the landscape nursery business," he says, "and a co-worker chanced upon a huge rose covering a chain-link fence beside the road. He made an unauthorized 'rustle,' bringing back flowers and cuttings, and urged me to go look. My immediate response was that any shrub that beautiful and self-reliant must have landscape potential. After a rosarian identified it as 'Mermaid' (a yellow-flowered, repeat-blooming climber from 1918), I found it was not available in commerce. Soon, 'Mermaid' and the other survivors we stumbled across over the next couple of years became the foundation of the Antique Rose Emporium."

In 1984 Mike discovered there was an organized group of Texas Rose Rustlers and soon he was rustling with the best of them. The objective of the loosely organized group has always been to find roses that have survived abandoned homesteads, to take cuttings and to share the bounty with others. They never steal the actual bushes. Mike's initial criteria for the roses he collected were survival and usefulness. As he got more familiar with them, fragrance, resistance to predatory insects and diseases, and diversity of form also became important.

In an age when most public gardens exist through membership, development and generous donations, the Antique Rose Emporium is self-funded by the roses and other plants it sells locally, online and through a fascinating catalog. What the Emporium shares with the best of public gardens is outstanding landscaping, idea gardens and beautiful ways to garden with time-tested roses that are essentially carefree.

Based 80 miles northwest of Houston, the Antique Rose Emporium has a Brenham address but is actually located closer to Independence, founded in 1835, and the home of Sam Houston in the 1850s. Visitors from the city typically take in the Rose Emporium and on the way back stop in Brenham to shop at its bustling farmer's market. A second Antique Rose Emporium is based in San Antonio, complete with display gardens, water features and a large variety of old roses and companion plants.

STRUCTURES AT THE ANTIQUE ROSE EMPORIUM HONOR ALL THINGS OLD. SALVAGED WINDOWS ARE FEATURED IN THE GREENHOUSE AND POTTING SHED (OPPOSITE). NEARBY, THE HARISTON KITCHEN AND COTTAGE GARDEN, WITH ITS WINDMILL BACKDROP, LETS VISITORS STEP BACK IN TIME TO AROUND 1850 WHEN THIS PART OF TEXAS WAS BEING SETTLED. ELSEWHERE, AN OVER-SCALE RUSTIC WOOD ARBOR IS HOME TO AN EXTENSIVE DISPLAY OF OLD CLIMBING ROSES SUCH AS LADY BANKS WHITE FROM 1807 AND LADY BANKS YELLOW, 1824.

ACREAGE: 8 ACRES OF DISPLAY GARDENS AND RETAIL

SEASONAL BLOOMS: PEAK BLOOM TIMES IN SPRING AND FALL

OTHER ATTRACTIONS: A CHAPEL, HISTORIC DWELLING AND OTHER SHELTERS FOR SPECIAL EVENTS

ACROSS THE GARDENS FROM THE HARISTON KITCHEN, GERANIUMS COLOR THE GREENHOUSE AND POTTING SHED IN THE WINTER MONTHS. THESE AND OTHER LOCALLY ADAPTED AS WELL AS NATIVE PLANTS ARE AVAILABLE FOR SALE, ALONG WITH MORE THAN 300 DIFFERENT ANTIQUE ROSES THAT CAN ALSO BE PURCHASED ONLINE OR THROUGH AN ILLUSTRATED CATALOG.

The Antique Rose Emporium Chapel, built in 1998, can accommodate up to 150 people for weddings and other special occasions. The building includes elements salvaged from churches in the community; for example, a stained glass window over the tall front door came originally from England and is over a hundred years old. Native Texas wildflowers bloom in the adjoining meadow, backed by a hedge tapestry of old roses that perfume the air and provide habitat for birds and other wildlife.

BAYOU BEND GARDENS

According to Miss Ima Hogg, her first impression of these 14 acres along Buffalo Bayou was that they were "nothing but a dense thicket." Undaunted, she and her brothers William and Michael set out to build the pink stucco house and develop the gardens, beginning in 1927. While Houston architect John H. Staub worked on the house and landscape architects Pat Fleming and Albert Sheppard the gardens, Miss Hogg herself was the guiding light. The only daughter of James Stephen Hogg, Texas' first native-born governor, she was an ardent student of architecture, the decorative arts, music, landscape architecture and garden design.

Miss Hogg envisioned outdoor garden rooms that were extensions of the house itself, places that were inviting to be in, literally for living, rather than to be seen only from indoor vantage points. She also wanted to preserve some of the wildness toward the outer reaches of the property, for dramatic contrast to the intensely cultivated grounds—as habitat for native plants and wildlife. The ravines southeast of the house offer proof that, contrary to legend, Houston is not uniformly flat as a pancake.

Most of the gardens at Bayou Bend were set in place by 1942. Miss Hogg became a member of the River Oaks Garden Club in 1928, a year after its founding, and in 1934 Bayou Bend was included in the Club's first and by now fabled Azalea Trail. Miss Hogg's active participation in the River Oaks Garden Club, an affiliate of the Garden Club of America, led to friendships with others who were passionate about gardening and landscaping. She traveled widely, visiting gardens and nurseries, and when a new plant caught her eye, every effort was made to make it happy in Houston—despite the sultry summers, poorly drained alkaline soil and the occasional blue norther, a fast-moving cold front accompanied by high winds and rapidly falling temperatures.

Soon after Miss Hogg donated her home and its priceless collection of American decorative arts to Houston's Museum of Fine Arts in 1957, she invited the River Oaks Garden Club to assume permanent supervision of the gardens. Thanks to each succeeding generation, the club's volunteers donate time, talent and resources to keep the grounds shipshape, as though Miss Hogg were expected at any moment. She would surely be pleased to know that through the efforts of the curator of the gardens and the members of the River Oaks Garden Club, the Bayou Bend gardens stand as the state's only formal organic public garden.

THE BOXWOOD PARTERRE SETTING FOR THE CLIO GARDEN WAS INSTALLED IN 1927-1928 WHILE THE HOUSE WAS BEING BUILT. AT MISS HOGG'S DIRECTION, THE DOME-SHAPED YAUPON HOLLIES WERE ADDED IN 1966. SURROUNDING BEDS FEATURE BLUE PANSIES IN WINTER, WHITE INDICA AZALEAS IN THE SPRING, FOLLOWED BY WISTERIA. THE CARRARA MARBLE STATUE OF CLIO, ONE OF THE SISTER-GODDESSES OF ARTS AND SCIENCES, REFERENCES MISS HOGG'S PASSION FOR HISTORY.

ACREAGE: 13 ACRES

SEASONAL BLOOMS: Azaleas, magnolias, roses in the spring

OTHER ATTRACTIONS: Tour of house, renown for decorative arts collection

The Diana Garden defines classical simplicity in the manner of Italian Renaissance gardens. Evergreen Japanese yews and yaupon holly hedges show off seasonal flowers, all in pink to complement the color of the house: magnolias in February, azaleas in March and April, and crape myrtles in June and July. This view of the Diana Garden toward the north terrace shows Miss Hogg's gift for dynamic integration of house and garden.

Tall pines, elms and oaks in
the Bayou Woodlands shelter
under-story flowering dogwoods and redbuds which, in
turn, complement the wild
flowers Miss Hogg loved to
encourage and the myriad
azaleas and camellias she
planted. The 'Duchesse de Caze'

pink camellias Miss Hogg
obtained from Avery Island in
Louisiana are among the first
japonica camellias ever grown
in Houston.

The Topiary Garden, given by the River Oaks Garden Club in celebration of the United States Bicentennial in 1976, displays five creatures of Miss Hogg's choosing: a turkey, squirrel, rabbit, deer and eagle. The topiaries—made from wire frames stuffed with sphagnum moss and planted with fig ivy—encircle a brick-paved garden centered by a big star of clipped dwarf yaupon holly for Texas, the Lone Star State.

THE FANCIFUL BUTTERFLY GARDEN WAS FIRST PLANTED WITH YELLOW AND PURPLE PANSIES, THEN, AFTER A TIME, MISS HOGG DECIDED CLIPPED BOXWOOD BORDERS FRAMING DWARF EVERGREEN AZALEAS WOULD MAKE A MORE ENDURING SHOW. FOUR CULTIVARS OF KURUME HYBRID AZALEAS— 'CHRISTMAS CHEER,' 'CORAL BELLS,' 'HEXE' AND 'HINO-DE-GIRI'—ARE PLANTED IN SWEEPS OF RED AND PINK. CAMELLIAS NEXT TO BENCHES ON EITHER SIDE BLOOM IN THE WINTER.

TODAY, THE CLIO IS THE FIRST GARDEN ENCOUNTERED BY VISITORS TO BAYOU BEND, AND IT IS ALSO ONE OF THE FIRST ON WHICH MISS HOGG APPLIED WHAT SHE KNEW ABOUT THE ART AND PRACTICE OF GARDENING. THE CAREFUL RECORDS SHE KEPT OF HER SUCCESSES AND FAILURES ARE TESTIMONY TO MISS HOGG'S PASSION FOR GETTING THINGS RIGHT. THE ORIGINAL PLANTINGS OF ROSES AND PERENNIAL FLOWERS SOON GAVE WAY TO BOX HEDGING THAT EMPHASIZES THE GEOMETRIC DESIGN EVERY DAY OF THE YEAR. ROSES THAT THRIVE IN HOUSTON'S TROPICAL SUMMERS HAVE BEEN RECENTLY REINTRODUCED TO THE CIRCULAR BEDS.

WITH STATUES OF THREE GREEK GODDESSES IN THE GARDENS AT BAYOU BEND, IT SEEMS INEVITABLE THAT MISS HOGG WOULD CULTIVATE THE VELVETY WHITE, SEDUCTIVELY ROMANTIC GARDENIA IN THE WHITE GARDEN. GETTING THE BUSHES TO GROW IN THE ENDEMIC POOR, ALKALINE SOIL COULD NOT HAVE BEEN EASY. HOWEVER, ALVIN WHEELER, HER GARDENER FOR 30 YEARS, HELPED OVERCOME SUCH OBSTACLES AND IN 1971 MISS HOGG DEDICATED THIS PART OF THE GARDEN TO HIM. BESIDES GARDENIAS, THERE ARE CAMELLIAS, TULIPS, NARCISSUS, IRIS, DOGWOOD, MOCK ORANGE, ANTIQUE ROSES, CALLA LILIES AND VIBURNUMS— TO NAME A FEW OF HER FAVORITES.

BEAUMONT BOTANICAL GARDENS

Little more than an hour's drive northeast of Houston, greater Beaumont is home to nearly a half million people. When the Beaumont Council of Garden Clubs organized on April 12, 1951, to develop a public garden center, the area had only a fraction of that population, but the founders had a clear vision.

Not until 1968, however, did the Council succeed in getting the City of Beaumont to set aside a portion of 500-acre Tyrrell Park for this purpose. Soon the Beaumont Garden Center building was constructed, using bricks salvaged from the Southern Pacific Railroad passenger station. Funded by Christmas house tours the Council initiated in 1964, it was finally dedicated August 20, 1971, 20 years from the time the seed of the idea was planted.

After adopting a master plan in 1972, the first order of the day was to identify and label the trees, shrubs and vines on the property. A Friendship Path through the garden was laid in 1977, and a Fragrance Garden was dedicated the following year. A Spring Tour of Private Gardens was added in 1986 as a second annual fund-raiser and almost every year since a new garden has been added, sponsored by the Council or other groups.

The Garden Center became the Beaumont Botanical Gardens in 1996 and today it includes, besides the previously mentioned gardens, the following: Green and White Garden, Stream Bed Garden, Antique Rose Garden, Grandmother's Garden, Modern Rose Garden, Japanese Garden, Azalea Trail, Daylily Display Garden, Native Plant Garden, Bromeliad Display Garden, Herb Garden, Camellia Garden, Secret Garden, and Palm and Agave Garden. The Horticultural Center, at the entrance to the Conservatory, was dedicated February 14, 2000, and in June that year, a fountain and "star" garden were added.

Modest fees are charged to tour the Conservatory, but access to the gardens is free every day during daylight hours. All garden paths are wheelchair and stroller accessible and there are welcoming benches and shelters placed all along the pathways that connect the gardens. Birders love the place and a small pond is home to ducks, turtles and Japanese Imperial koi that visiting children take delight in feeding.

The annual Spring Garden Tour of commendable private gardens is held the first weekend in May and the Christmas Tour of Homes the first Friday in December. Plant sales held in conjunction with the tours add to the funds raised and help make it possible to maintain and continually improve remarkable gardens that are truly public, in that no admission is charged (other than to the Conservatory).

BROMELIADS, ORCHIDS AND PLUMERIAS GROW WITH TROPICAL ABANDON IN THE WARREN LOOSE CONSERVATORY, THE SECOND LARGEST IN A PUBLIC GARDEN IN THE STATE OF TEXAS. NAMED TO HONOR AN AVID PLANTSMAN, THE 10,000-SQUARE-FOOT SPACE HAS A POOL FOR KOI, A WATERFALL AND A PLAZA WITH ARBOR.

ACREAGE: 23.5 ACRES

SEASONAL BLOOMS: CAMELLIAS IN WINTER-EARLY SPRING; AZALEAS IN EARLY SPRING; ANTIQUE ROSES IN SPRING

OTHER ATTRACTIONS: THE BOTANICAL GARDENS ARE SITED WITHIN 500-ACRE TYRRELL PARK WITH GOLF COURSE, EQUESTRIAN AND NATURE TRAILS

The Azalea Trail, dedicated in 1991, is a place of breathtaking beauty in early spring, usually beginning late February and continuing into April. Mature trees on the site add grandeur that comes only with age. Not only do they bring welcome shade in the hot summers—for azaleas as well as people—but their foliage masses give a boost of oxygen that subtly lifts the spirits of gardeners and visitors alike.

A BIRDHOUSE EXPRESSED AS A COUNTRY CHURCH (LEFT) ADDS A CHARMING TOUCH TO A WOODED AREA. THE JAPANESE GARDEN (ABOVE) WAS ADDED IN 1991, COMPLETE WITH A *torii* GATE THAT IN JAPAN WOULD BE FOUND AT THE ENTRY TO A *Shinto* SHRINE, BUT ALSO AT BUDDHIST TEMPLES. LOUISIANA AND WATER IRIS OPEN THEIR DELICATELY COLORED FLOWERS IN THE SPRING AND CAN BE ADMIRED FROM THE BRIDGE.

A crane statue (opposite, far left) is bathed by the waterfall in the Conservatory. Bromeliads, decorative members of the pineapple family, have vividly colored leaves and thrive in the same conditions as orchids.

Calla lilies (left) grow in beds outdoors as well as in the Conservatory and often bloom at Easter, along with the displays of Easter lilies (above) that visitors look forward to in the spring.

BELL PARK CACTI GARDENS

When the Panhandle Plains folk of Hale City and Epworth decided to unite their towns in 1893, buildings from both were moved to the new town site, which they named Hale Center. Ranching was the order of the day until the development of widespread irrigation in the 20th century. Today more than 400,000 acres, all irrigated, produce cotton, grain sorghum, wheat, sunflowers, sugar beets and table vegetables.

The Bell Park Cacti Garden, which stands tellingly at the intersection of two Farm-to-Market roads, FM 1424 and FM 1914, was established to honor a revered authority on agronomy and range management, Hershell Bell. The gently rolling terrain contains more than 350 specimens representing at least 15 different species of cacti and other succulents. The Hale Center sits at an altitude of 2,112 feet, and the United States Department of Agriculture Hardiness Zone Map places it in Zone 6, which indicates winter low temperatures of 0 to -10 degrees. Cacti and other succulents are typically associated with warm, dry climates, but many are hardy to 0 and some to well below.

Bell Park can be experienced by wandering the path and, should the mood and good weather strike at the same time, picnic tables are available. While occasional weeds must be pulled, this is essentially a carefree garden—no watering, no deadheading, no fussing over predatory insects or diseases. As an example of the Xeriscape concept, pure and simple—to set no garden in motion that will require undue amounts of irrigation during normal periods of drought—Bell Park Cacti Garden gets five stars.

Some of the plants that grow in Bell Park include various agaves; species of small cacti called coryphantha that grow three or four inches wide near the ground; echinocereus such as *Echinocereus coccineus*, known as Texas hedgehog; species of escobaria, small and clump-forming cacti; many prickly pears or opuntias; mountain ball cactus or *Pediocactus simpsonii*; and yuccas such as Adam's needle and the related Texas red yucca (*Hesperaloe parviflora*) and the rock lily or Texas tuberose (*Manfreda maculosa*).

SPIKY AGAVES AND YUCCAS STAND IN STARK CONTRAST TO THE CHOLLA CACTUS WITH ITS MANY GANGLY AND EVEN GOOFY LOOKING BRANCHES.

ACREAGE: 1/3 ACRE

SEASONAL BLOOMS: SPRING, OR FOLLOWING RAIN

OTHER ATTRACTIONS: THE HALE COUNTY FARM AND RANCH MUSEUM IS NEARBY

Opuntia imbricata VARIETY ARBORESCENS, A TREE CHOLLA (RIGHT UPPER) HAS CHAIN-LIKE BRANCHES AND CAN GROW LARGE AND SHRUB-LIKE TO 15 FEET. THE PINCUSHION CACTI FORM CLUMPS TO A FOOT OR MORE ACROSS AND OF SIMILAR HEIGHT. THERE ARE A VAST NUMBER OF OPUNTIAS OR PRICKLY-PEAR CACTI (OPPOSITE UPPER), FAVORED IN DRY GARDENS FOR THEIR SPECTACULAR FLOWERS. YUCCA PLANTS (OPPOSITE LOWER) ARE APPRECIATED FOR THEIR YEAR-ROUND BOLD, GRAPHIC APPEARANCE IN THE GARDEN; TWO-INCH WAXY WHITE FLOWERS THAT PERFUME THE AIR CLUSTER ON STURDY STEMS TO 4 FEET HIGH IN THE SPRING.

BRACKENRIDGE PARK
JAPANESE TEA GARDEN

Situated about two miles north of downtown San Antonio, Brackenridge Park's nearly 350 acres are home to the San Antonio Zoo, and a 3.5-mile miniature railway and cableway for children, the Chinese Sunken Gardens, and the Japanese Tea Garden. Artesian springs north of the park feed the San Antonio River, which winds past the paved paths for walkers and bicyclists. There are opportunities for picnicking, pedal boating, fishing, birding and interacting with nature. Finally, Brackenridge Golf Course, the oldest municipal golf course in Texas, is sited within the park.

Other than the Zoo, the Japanese Tea Gardens are one of the most popular features in Brackenridge Park. They offer escape to another world, one with shaded retreats, intricately crafted stone bridges and pillars and a dramatic 60-foot waterfall that splashes into the ponds where birds and turtles gather for sustenance.

The tea ceremony and its practice in a garden setting originated in China eons ago, but migrated to Japan where it has become highly ritualized as an exercise in courtesy and art. Deeply rooted in Zen Buddhism, nothing about the Japanese tea garden or the tea ceremony is superficial or accidental. Every thing and every movement has meaning. The garden's seasonal blooms symbolize the Japanese celebration of the new life in spring, evidenced by the flowering of the cherry trees and the azaleas; and, in autumn, the approaching winter is embodied by the exquisite beauty of a Japanese cut-leaf maple's gloriously colored foliage. No rock or stone is casually placed; in the Japanese tradition, the garden's maker quietly placed his hands on each stone and asked where it wished to be placed.

Simplicity is the essence of a Japanese Tea Garden, the embodiment of the notion that less is more—and yes, there are Texans who find majesty in the subtle, the small, the understated—who come here to let themselves be mesmerized by nature's beauty.

The Japanese Tea Gardens are open year-round. Admittance is charged for the Zoo, but not to the park and Tea Gardens.

FALLEN BLOSSOMS OF THE CORAL TREE (*Erythrina crista-galli*) FLOATING IN A POND IN THE TEA GARDEN ARE AN ELOQUENT EXAMPLE OF *shibui*, A JAPANESE WORD THAT CANNOT BE EXACTLY TRANSLATED TO ENGLISH BUT WHICH MEANS APPROXIMATELY "EXQUISITE BEAUTY." WHILE WESTERNERS MAY SEE FALLEN PETALS AS SPENT OR DEAD, EASTERN THOUGHT PLACES THEM AS TRANSCENDENT IN THE CIRCLE OF LIFE.

ACREAGE: 343.7 ACRES
SEASONAL BLOOMS: PRIMARILY SPRING AND FALL
OTHER ATTRACTIONS: MANY RECREATIONAL FEATURES AND CHINESE SUNKEN GARDEN

INTRICATELY LAID STONE WALLS AND COLUMNS (OPPOSITE PAGE) FRAME THE GARDENS AND SUPPORT SHELTER FROM SUN AND RAIN. JAPANESE STONE MASONS CONSULT EACH STONE AS TO WHERE IT WISHES TO BE PLACED, THUS LENDING MYSTERIOUS ENERGY TO THE HUMAN EXPERIENCE OF PLACE.

'TANGERINE BEAUTY' BEGNONIA (LEFT, UPPER), ALSO KNOWN AS CROSS-VINE AND TRUMPET VINE, GROWS RAPIDLY TO COVER ALMOST ANY SUPPORTING STRUCTURE AND BLOOMS PROFUSELY IN THE SPRING AND AGAIN IN THE FALL. IT IS EVERGREEN AND THE FLOWERS ATTRACT HUMMINGBIRDS.

RUSTIC FENCING ALONG A BOARDWALK (LEFT) LEADS TO THE JAPANESE TEA HOUSE. THE DIFFERENT ELEVATIONS AND THE GARDENS LET VISITORS DISCOVER DIFFERENT VIEWS AND EMPHASIZE THE EXPERIENTIAL ASPECT OF THE LANDSCAPE.

The intense blue flowers of *Thunbergia erecta* (RIGHT, UPPER) STAND SURROUNDED BY THE FRESH GREEN OF FERN FRONDS. WHILE MOST *thunbergias* ARE VINES (BLACK-EYED SUSAN VINE, FOR EXAMPLE), THE SPECIES ERECTA IS MORE LIKE A SHRUB.

THE FLOWERS OF THE CORAL TREE ARE WAXY AND LONG-LASTING. THEY ALSO ARE RICH IN NECTAR AND A GREAT ATTRACTION TO HUMMINGBIRDS.

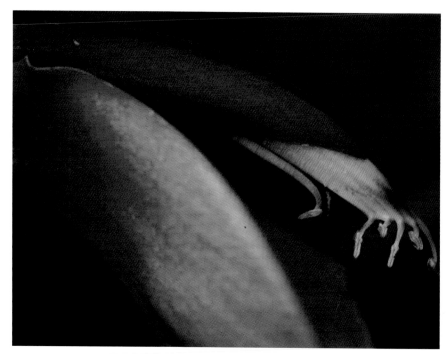

THE STONE WORK IN THE JAPANESE TEA GARDENS (OPPOSITE PAGE) HAS AN OTHER-WORLDLY QUALITY THAT STIRS THE IMAGINATION. WHILE THE WATERS HERE ARE STILL AND REFLECTIVE, NEARBY IS A 60-FOOT WATERFALL THAT FILLS THE AIR WITH SOUND AND ENERGY.

CHANDOR GARDENS

Driving west from Fort Worth, the arid terrain along the 30 miles or so to Weatherford gives hardly a clue that in this town of 25,000 there is an English-style garden graced with unexpected touches of chinoiserie. Douglas Chandor, its originator, was a gifted portrait painter who came to America from Surrey, England, in 1926, married Ina Huetman in 1934 and settled here in her hometown.

Beginning in 1936, the Chandors built the gardens, a 16-year odyssey of re-shaping the land and adapting English ideas about gardening to suit the local climate. Strong structural details that divide the landscape into 18 different rooms are softened by bounteous plantings, water features and a quirky penchant for Chinese architecture and ornamentation.

Turning the barren land—excepting some cactus—into beautiful gardens was no task for trowels and pruning shears. It took picks, shovels and yes, dynamite, not to mention a healthy dose of fortitude to construct Chandor's vision of a "living artwork."

While Chandor painted portraits of such notables as Queen Elizabeth, Winston Churchill, and Presidents Herbert Hoover and Franklin Roosevelt, his achievements as a garden maker are perhaps more remarkable. Although he died in 1953, his widow kept the gardens open to the public until her death in 1978, after which they fell to neglect. Fortunately, the City of Weatherford purchased the property in 2002 and set about restoring Chandor Gardens, so that today it is a favorite place for family outings, retreats, weddings and other social events.

An example of Chandor's creativity may be found in the green bottle glass that surrounds the dragon fountain. He was clearly practicing adaptive re-use of materials otherwise destined for landfill long before the idea became a mantra for anyone striving to be "green." In fact, recycled glass as a colorful groundcover has recently been featured as an avant-garde idea at the garden festival held annually in the summer at Chateau de Chaumont in the Loire Valley of France.

Chandor Gardens, with its 5,600-square-foot dwelling sited on 3.5 acres, is located in the heart of Weatherford's historic district. Experience the different gardens by following meandering paths that promise surprises at every turn, different views, and the fragrances of seasonal flowers. Exuberant sounds from the 30-foot waterfall are counterbalanced by quietly soothing fountains. Private gardens on this grand scale often, if not usually, die with their owners. That this one is alive and well is testimony to the genius of its makers and to the goodness of the Weatherford townsfolk.

CHANDOR WAS BOLD IN BRINGING A ROCK-EDGED STREAM RIGHT UP TO THE HOUSE, SO IT COULD BE ENJOYED FROM A COMFORTABLE PLACE EVEN IN THE DOG DAYS OF SUMMER. THE WHITE BRIDGE, WITH ITS DISTINCTIVE POST FINIALS, IS FULL OF THE SYMBOLISM OF TRANSCENDENCE—AND PROVIDES A FAVORITE SPOT FOR WEDDING PHOTOS.

ACREAGE: 3.5 ACRES

SEASONAL BLOOMS: APRIL TO NOVEMBER

OTHER ATTRACTIONS: ELEGANTLY APPOINTED DWELLING

THE DRAGON FOUNTAIN (ABOVE), BUILT IN THE 1940S, USES CHI-LING STATUES FOUND IN NEW YORK CITY. SURROUNDING IT ARE COLORFUL BOTTLES, MARBLES, AND CERAMIC TILES HANDMADE BY THE ARTIST. THE SUNKEN SITE WAS FIRST SEEN AS SUITED FOR A SWIMMING POOL, BUT CHANDOR ENVISIONED SOMETHING MORE GRAND. AN IVY-COVERED STONE WALL AND STEPPING STONES OF HIS DESIGN RING THE FOUNTAIN.

A CHINESE LANTERN (OPPOSITE, UPPER LEFT) STANDS SENTRY NEAR THE BASE OF THE 30-FOOT WATERFALL. DELICATE APPEARING BUT HARDY FERNS GROW BETWEEN THE ROCKS. IVY-CLAD WALLS (OPPOSITE, LOWER LEFT) LINE AN INVITING STONE AND BRICK STAIRWAY THAT LEADS TO YET ANOTHER MAGIC PLACE—ONE OF 18 DISTINCT SPACES OR "ROOMS" IN THE 3.5-ACRE GARDEN. EVERGREENS FRONTED BY SEASONAL COLOR—HERE VIOLAS AND PANSIES IN THE SPRINGTIME— FRAME THE HOUSE, WITH ITS DISTINCTIVE ITALIANATE PORTICO. CONIFERS SUCH AS JUNIPERS AND ARBORVITAE THRIVE IN THE OFTEN HARSH CLIMATE AND PROVIDE GREEN EVEN IN THE DEAD OF WINTER.

CHANDOR'S GIFT AS A GARDEN
DESIGNER IS THAT HE SUCCESSFULLY
UNITED SQUARE AND CURVING
SPACES, BOTH FROM ONE GARDEN
ROOM TO ANOTHER, AND JUXTA-
POSED NEXT TO THE HOUSE.
STONE STRUCTURES INSPIRED BY
THOSE IN CHINESE IMPERIAL
GARDENS ARE SEEN HERE, AT THE
SITE OF WHAT TODAY MIGHT BE
CALLED A RAIN GARDEN, THE
"GREEN" SOLUTION FOR A PIECE OF
GROUND THAT IS POORLY DRAINED.

CHARLES UMLAUF SCULPTURE GARDEN

When he was but a lad, Charles Julius Umlauf's fourth grade teacher recognized him as artistically gifted and introduced him to professors at the Art Institute of Chicago who were similarly impressed and granted him summer scholarships. Graduation from high school was followed by further studies at the Art Institute and at the Chicago School of Sculpture. Following his 1937 marriage to Angeline Allen, a fellow student at the Art Institute, the couple settled in Austin where Umlauf was to be an instructor in sculpture at the University of Texas for the next 40 years, until he retired in 1981 as professor emeritus. In 1984 the Umlaufs gave their home and studio with sculptures and other works of art to the Umlauf Sculpture Garden and Museum.

The light of talent that glowed in the schoolboy Umlauf never dimmed, it simply grew brighter throughout his life. He sculpted with virtuosity, from detailed realism to lyrical abstractionism and worked in practically any medium he could get his hands on—exotic woods, terra cotta, cast stone, bronze, alabaster and marble. He was particularly fond of sculpting mothers and offspring, mythological and religious figures, sensuous nudes and playful animals.

Umlauf's work has more public placements in Texas than that of any other sculptor, and can also be seen in such prestigious places as the Smithsonian in Washington, D.C., and the Metropolitan Museum in New York City. However, it is here in the museum and gardens named in his honor where 130 sculptures, drawings and paintings constitute an inspiring tour de force. While admittance fees and donations keep the doors open, in fulfilling the institution's mission "to provide educational experiences and programs that encourage the appreciation and understanding sculpture," free admission is offered to all school groups.

The garden's six acres are defined by a large oval gravel path surrounding a "Y," also detailed in gravel paths, altogether forming the international symbol for peace. A brook bisects the Y, and a pond at each end has an island with a sculpture. Wooden bridges facilitate crossing the brook at two points. The sculptures have been masterfully placed, so that they can be seen at some distance from the path and then approached by way of several different surfaces—concrete, brick, grass, gravel—for closer inspection.

The Umlauf offers a variety of learning experiences for persons of all ages and regularly showcases new works by visiting artists. The gardens themselves are primarily green and natural, maintained so as to quietly provide a home for the sculptures rather than an intensely cultivated landscape.

"THE KISS" IS ONE OF MORE THAN 50 SCULPTURES BY CHARLES UMLAUF ON DISPLAY IN THE GARDENS. THE 6-ACRE SITE HAS OPEN AREAS OF LAWNS BACKDROPPED BY TOWERING OLD SHADE TREES.

ACREAGE: 6 ACRES

SEASONAL BLOOMS: PRIMARILY SPRING IN THIS TREE-SHADED GARDEN

OTHER ATTRACTIONS: INDOOR EXHIBITIONS IN A MODERN MUSEUM

THE BROOK HAS AN ISLAND AT
EACH END WHERE A SINGLE
STATUE IS DISPLAYED, HERE
UMLAUF'S FAMOUS "SPIRIT OF
FLIGHT." OTHER SCULPTURES—
HUMAN, ANIMAL, ABSTRACTIONS—
ARE PLACED THROUGHOUT THE
GARDENS, EACH WHERE IT SEEMS
MOST AT HOME.

Umlauf's "Pieta," cast in bronze in 1947, depicts Christ, his mother Mary and Mary Magdalene. Umlauf's wife was the model for Mary. Benches have been placed throughout the gardens to invite visitors to sit quietly and contemplate the sculptures in their natural setting.

UMLAUF'S "ST. FRANCIS WITH
BIRDS" IS A LIFE-SIZE BRONZE
CAST IN 1972, HONORING
ST. FRANCIS OF ASSISI, WHO IS
REPUTED TO HAVE SO LOVED
NATURE THAT HE ONCE PREACHED
TO A FLOCK OF SPARROWS.

UMLAUF'S "CRUCIFIXION" WAS
CAST OF ALUMINUM IN 1948 AND
STANDS ON A BLACK GRANITE
BASE. THE SCULPTURE IS
APPROXIMATELY 10.5 FEET TALL.
THE FLOWERS IN THE FOREGROUND
BELONG TO THE RED BUCKEYE, A
TEXAS NATIVE.

CLARK GARDENS BOTANICAL PARK

An hour or so west of Fort Worth, down a country lane between Weatherford and Mineral Wells, lies a world-class treasure—the 143-acre Clark Gardens Botanical Park. Begun as the private garden of Max and Billie Clark in 1972, which they expressed in traditional landscaping on the rugged Texas hillside, it was donated by them to a non-profit organization named in their honor in 1999. Clark Gardens opened to the public the following year.

Today the 35 acres devoted to 50 different cultivated gardens are a model of environmental awareness, demonstrated by the extensive use of Texas native plants and non-natives that have proven adaptable, set out in sustainable landscapes that are not dependent on irrigation during normal periods of dry weather. Low maintenance is also a constant consideration as new plantings and features are added.

Not only are these gardens places for flowers, trees and shrubs, but they are also rich in wildlife. Butterflies begin to appear in February and are everywhere by March. Birdsong and the buzzing of bees can be heard daily and in autumn, visitors are treated to the migrations of Monarch butterflies, ducks and geese. Waterfalls, ponds and lakes are home to black and white swans, as well as blue herons and great egrets. If lucky, you may see the peacocks show off their plumage in the park.

Of particular note to kids of all ages are the three different G-Scale Model Garden Trains that ply the landscape on 700 feet of track, complete with seven-foot-high trestles fashioned from willow, waterfalls and small streams. Scaled-down buildings at "Clark Station" are cunningly made from plant materials—poppy seed heads, vine tendrils, cinnamon sticks, pinecone scales and acorns.

Clark Gardens Botanical Park is a model for what a public garden needs to be in the 21st century. It has beautiful design, locally adapted plantings that thrive with a minimum of fuss, and lots of places for people to enjoy themselves—from quiet moments of meditation or even napping, to lively hikes to observe the wildlife, as well as family picnics, or life celebrations. The park makes an ideal setting for graduation parties and proms, weddings, anniversaries—and even business and personal growth seminars and retreats. Anyone with the slightest appreciation for natural beauty is sure to find something extraordinary any day and any season of the year at Clark Gardens.

IN LATE WINTER AND SPRING, PANSIES IN YELLOW, BLUE-PURPLE AND RASPBERRY ABOUND ALONG THE ORCHARD GARDEN'S CRUSHED BRICK WALKWAYS. THE FLOWERING REDBUD IS BUT ONE OF MANY TREES AND SHRUBS THAT FILL CLARK GARDENS WITH BLOOM AT THE BEGINNING OF THE GARDENING SEASON: AZALEA, MEXICAN PLUM, LILAC, MAGNOLIA, QUINCE—NOT TO MENTION CEDAR WAX WINGS EN MASSE.

ACREAGE: 35 ACRES

SEASONAL BLOOMS: Late winter/early spring: daffodils, flowering trees, azaleas; spring: lilacs, roses, iris, daylilies, perennials; summer: water lilies, cannas, crape myrtle; fall: chrysanthemums, roses, ornamental grasses; winter: Holly berries

OTHER ATTRACTIONS: Historic house in the park's West Garden area; G-scale model garden trains

DISTINCTIVE EVERGREEN CONIFER TREES LEND A CERTAIN MYSTERY TO THE CHANNEL GARDEN SETTING. THE SYMMETRY, SPLASHING FOUNTAINS AND REFLECTING POOL SPEAK FLUENTLY IN THE LANGUAGE OF CLASSIC GARDEN DESIGN, DATING BACK HUNDREDS OF YEARS. IN A CLIMATE ALMOST CERTAIN TO BE HOT AND DRY IN SUMMER, GARDENERS DEPEND ON WATER FEATURES FOR COOLING SIGHTS AND SOUNDS.

VISITORS TO THE METAL-ROOFED CHAPEL (SEEN IN THE PHOTOGRAPH ABOVE) CAN ENJOY A STROLL THROUGH AN ARBOR THAT IS COMPLETELY COVERED WITH THE TALL ARCHING CANES OF LADY BANKS ROSES. AT THEIR MOMENT OF GLORY IN EARLY SPRING, HARDLY ANYTHING CAN BE SEEN EXCEPT COUNTLESS YELLOW OR WHITE ROSES THAT PERFUME THE AIR WITH THE DELICATE SCENT OF THE TRUE ENGLISH VIOLET (*Viola odorata*).

LADY BANKS ROSES SHELTER AN ARBOR IN ALL SEASONS, OFFERING LEAFY SHADE IN SUMMER AND FALL, ADMITTING WELCOME SUN RAYS IN WINTER AND TURNING INTO A BOWER OF VIOLET-SCENTED BLOSSOMS IN SPRING. BOTH THE

YELLOW AND WHITE FORMS OF *Rosa banksiae*, A NEARLY THORNLESS, MOSTLY EVERGREEN SPECIES FROM WESTERN CHINA, GROW HERE.

SWEET WILLIAM AND OTHER DIANTHUS (OPPOSITE, CLOCKWISE FROM UPPER LEFT) OFFER COLOR AND CLOVE SCENT IN SPRING AND EARLY SUMMER; DAFFODILS AND OTHER NARCISSUS HERALD THE END OF WINTER; GOBLET-SHAPED

TULIPS TOAST A PERFECT SPRING DAY; ORANGE WALLFLOWERS AND BLUE-PURPLE PANSIES SHOW HOW OPPOSITES ON THE COLOR WHEEL ATTRACT AND COMPLEMENT.

CULLEN SCULPTURE GARDEN AT THE MUSEUM OF FINE ARTS, HOUSTON

The Cullen Sculpture Garden's green acre in the heart of Houston is one of the finest sculpture gardens in the world. Designed by Isamu Noguchi, it provides a showcase for modernist masterworks in a setting of native Texas trees and shrubs. Though small in terms of actual square feet, it feels large, with horizontal expanses of paving and lawns counterbalanced by plinth-like walls. Each sculpture can be contemplated alone in its setting without visual intrusion of other works. And, remarkably, admission to the Cullen Sculpture Garden is free.

The Sculpture Garden had its beginnings in 1968-1969 when the Brown Foundation, Inc., provided the funds to purchase two city blocks across the street from the Museum. While visiting the Israel Museum in Jerusalem in 1970, Alice Pratt Brown, one of the benefactors, took note of Noguchi's design for the 5-acre urban space, and recommended that he be engaged to design the garden.

It would be 1976 before Noguchi made his first visit to Houston. Three years later his maquette of the Cullen Sculpture Garden was presented to the community and while responses were diverse, the plan was ultimately approved. Opening ceremonies on April 5, 1986, attracted more than 6,500 visitors.

For help with the landscaping, Noguchi wisely turned to a legendary Houston garden designer, Johnny Steele. More than 80 trees canopy the garden today, mostly Texas natives, including Drummond red maples, mimosa, loblolly pines, Drake elms, bald cypress, Southern magnolia, crape myrtle and water oaks. There are also plantings of giant timber bamboo, feather bamboo, green pittosporum (but not the variegated form), evergreen wisteria and Asian jasmine. Live oaks and cedar elms grow along the garden's outer walls.

Aside from Noguchi's sensitive design, the success of the Cullen Sculpture Garden owes a great deal to the narrowly focused intent, to display the works of "artists who have shaped the course of sculpture in the 20th century." Commissioned works by Houston artists include "Houston Triptych" by Ellsworth Kelly and "Can Johnny Come Out and Play?" by Jim Love. Other artists whose sculptures can be contemplated at the Cullen include Emile-Antoine Bourdelle, Louise Bourgeois, Alexander Calder, Tony Cragg, Mark Di Suvero, Alberto Giacometti, Joseph Havel, Bryan Hunt, Henry Laurens, Jacques Lipchitz, Marino Marini, Aristide Maillol, Joan Miro, Richard Serra, Joel Shapiro, David Smith, Frank Stella and William Tucker.

ALEXANDER CALDER PAINTED STEEL "THE CRAB" (1962) HAS BEEN VARIOUSLY DESCRIBED BY ADULTS AS "LURKING" OR EVEN "MENACING," WHILE CHILDREN TYPICALLY FIND IT FUN—QUITE IN KEEPING WITH DESIGNER NOGUCHI'S WISH THAT THE GARDENS BE A "GEOMETRY OF PLAYFULNESS." WHETHER "THE CRAB" SEEMS FRIENDLY OR ON THE VERGE OF ATTACKING IS ALSO AFFECTED BY THE TIME OF DAY AND WEATHER CONDITIONS.

ACREAGE: A LITTLE OVER 1 (EXTRAORDINARY) ACRE

SEASONAL BLOOMS: QUIETLY GREEN YEAR-ROUND

OTHER ATTRACTIONS: THE MUSEUM OF FINE ARTS AND THE GLASSELL SCHOOL OF ART

DAVID SMITH'S STAINLESS STEEL
"TWO CIRCLE SENTINEL" (1961)
IS EVOCATIVE OF A ROBOT, WHICH
CAN BE INTERPRETED AS HAPPY
AND OUTGOING ON A SUNNY DAY,
SAD AND WITHDRAWN WHEN THE
WEATHER TURNS WET AND GLOOMY.

Frank Stella's steel and bronze "Decanter" (1987) is a collage of forms that seems to burst into space, as though paying homage to Houston's NASA Johnson Space Center.

Designer Noguchi envisioned a place where the artworks would engage in a dialogue with the garden and visitors would interact with the sculptures. Rolling lawns and towering native trees complete the site as an oasis at the heart of Greater Houston, which has more square miles than any other American city.

THE DALLAS ARBORETUM

With the exception of the Netherlands, no place on earth has more tulips in March and April than the Dallas Arboretum (400,000 and counting)—which combine with a host of azaleas to make the largest spring flower festival in the Southwest. Since 1974, when the Dallas Arboretum and Botanical Society of Dallas incorporated as a non-profit institution, combining the 44-acre DeGolyer family esate and the 22-acre Camp family estate, the Arboretum has become one of the best designed public gardens in the country. There is truly something for all ages and persuasions—water features, formal gardens, nature walks, a Texas Pioneer adventure complete with an authentic native American tepee and innumerable places to picnic.

There are six principal gardens: Paseo de Flores, a central, meandering walkway; Jonnsson Color Garden, 6.5 acres with over 2,000 azaleas sheltered by flowering dogwoods and untold scores of tulips and daffodils, followed by cannas and caladiums in summer, chrysanthemums in the fall; the Palmer Fern Dell with a micro-fine mist system that makes it a welcome oasis in hot weather; A Woman's Garden, a 4.3-acre formal garden divided into several small garden rooms; the DeGolyer Gardens, 4.5 acres originally planted in 1940 that include an allee of towering magnolia trees; and the Lay Ornamental Gardens, a 2.2-acre Texas cottage garden.

In addition, there is the Martha Brooks Camellia Garden that blooms in winter with more than 200 camellias in 30 different cultivars. The Pecan Grove is a favorite place for picnickers and Toad Corners, at the terminus of Crape Myrtle Allee, has a quartet of giant bronze toads spouting 20-foot streams of water that kids go wild over when the weather turns hot. The 2.5-acre Texas Pioneer Adventure shows how plants were essential for pioneer survival. And finally, there is the secluded Nancy's Garden, with child-sized benches and a sculpture of little girls dancing entitled "Thank Heaven for Little Girls."

Each year brings three special events of note: Dallas Blooms, in March and April; Autumn at the Arboretum, September and October; and Holiday at the Arboretum, November and December. These are the months when the Arboretum's staff of 25 professional gardeners focuses their efforts on filling all the gardens with the season's most spectacular flowers and floral embellishments.

Plant research is an important part of the Arboretum's mission, the goal being to introduce plants uniquely suited to the gardens of North Texas. New varieties that pass muster qualify as Texas Superstar introductions, or gain distinction in the North Texas Winner's Circle. In addition, the Arboretum is an official testing site for All-America Selections, an independent organization that evaluates new annual flowers.

THIS TOPIARY 10-GALLON HAT OF PATRIOTICALLY PLANTED PETUNIAS, COMPLETE WITH THE STATE'S SIGNATURE STAR, IS PROOF THAT WHILE THINGS IN GENERAL ARE BIG IN TEXAS, THEY ARE EVEN BIGGER AT THE ARBORETUM. DEPENDING ON THE SEASON, OTHER TOPIARY-STYLE PLANTINGS INCLUDE 18-FOOT PEACOCKS, FLOWER-COVERED VOLKSWAGENS, GIANT PUMPKINS EXPRESSED WITH MARIGOLDS, AND ORANGE IMPATIENS, AND A THREE-LAYER BIRTHDAY CAKE THAT IS 15 FEET TALL.

ACREAGE: 66 ACRES

SEASONAL BLOOMS: EXCEPTIONAL LATE WINTER-EARLY SUMMER AND EARLY FALL THROUGH HOLIDAY EXHIBITIONS

OTHER ATTRACTIONS: CONCERT STAGE AND LAWN FOR LIVE THEATER AND MUSIC

CLIMBING ROSES BOWER AN ARBOR (OPPOSITE, UPPER) AND BRING THE SEASON'S FIRST WAVE OF BLOOMS IN APRIL WHEN THE ARBORETUM OFFERS WORKSHOPS IN HOW TO PROPAGATE HEIRLOOM ROSES FROM CUTTINGS. PETUNIAS (OPPOSITE, LOWER) ADD VIVID COLOR FOR MONTHS ON END; THEY THRIVE IN THE DRY AIR THAT PREVAILS IN THIS PART OF TEXAS AND REQUIRE LITTLE GROOMING TO LOOK THEIR BEST FOR EACH DAY'S VISITORS.

RED, WHITE AND BLUE PETUNIAS MAKE UP A LIVING STAR THAT TOWERS OVER THE HUMAN VISITORS NEXT TO A CORRAL OF LIFE-SIZE TOPIARY LONGHORNS AND PONIES, ALL BASED ON METAL FORMS THAT THE DALLAS ARBORETUM MAKES AVAILABLE FOR RENTAL TO OTHER PUBLIC GARDENS. TRADITIONAL TOPIARIES, SCULPTED BY SHEARING SHRUBS SUCH AS YEW AND BOXWOOD INTO GEOMETRICAL AND ANIMAL SHAPES, ALSO ADD DRAMA AND A TOUCH OF HUMOR TO THE LANDSCAPE.

EAST TEXAS ARBORETUM AND BOTANICAL SOCIETY

Located about 70 miles southeast of Dallas, the East Texas Arboretum has something for all ages and interests, from nature trails to formal gardens—all wheelchair and stroller friendly. Athens is considered to be the spot where prairie meets the East Texas Piney Woods—hilly, but not to be confused with the Texas Hill Country.

Built on the site of a long abandoned truck farm, the East Texas Arboretum and Botanical Society took a leap of faith and, having no money, no assets and few members, purchased the 100 acres in 1993 and the intensely dedicated volunteers got to work. Today the land is debt-free and the founders can look with pride on a thriving, ever improving institution.

The formal gardens are filled with many colors, textures and scents—especially from gardenias, magnolias and several different varieties of honeysuckle. There is a herb and medicinal garden at the Wofford House that evokes memories of what the pioneers in this part of Texas must have cultivated. Wofford House, which was built in 1850 in Fincastle, 20 miles southeast of Athens, and moved to the Arboretum in 2002, is now a museum, furnished with period pieces.

On the walking trails there is a 115-foot suspension bridge over Walnut Creek with banks lined with large ferns, honeysuckle and berry vines. A bog full of pitcher plants may be admired from an overlook platform, provided so as not to disturb the delicate ecosystem.

Besides the Wofford House, history buffs love the Little Red School House and the Miller Barn, a corn crib, complete with antique farm equipment. Children can't wait to visit the play garden sand pit, the slide in the hill, the playhouses and the fort.

For nature enthusiasts there are plantings of butterfly and bee plants, and several varieties of dragonfly live around the pond. There is also a busy beehive, and opportunities for birders abound. The typical visitor response is to remark on the peacefulness of the garden or to say that visiting is restorative to the soul. Even in the dog days of high summer sitting in one of the rocking chairs on the Wofford House dog-trot porch is said to be a "cool" experience.

Aside from the gardens and the nature trails, there is a 4,000 square foot Woman's Building, designed as a pavilion for classrooms and offices.

THE GEN MONKHOUSE "LITTLE RED SCHOOL HOUSE" IS NAMED FOR "A SWEET LADY IN TOWN WHO WANTED TO DO SOMETHING NICE FOR THE ARBORETUM BEFORE SHE PASSED AWAY." IT REPLICATES A ONE-ROOM SCHOOL TYPICAL OF THE LATE 1800s. IN SPRING THE PERENNIAL GARDEN BLOOMS WITH SELF-SEEDING LARKSPUR, EARLY DAYLILIES AND IMPATIENS IN THE SHADIER AREAS. THE WHEELCHAIR AND STROLLER ACCESSIBLE WALKWAYS ARE EXPOSED AGGREGATE.

ACREAGE: 100 ACRES

SEASONAL BLOOMS: LATE MARCH TO MID-OCTOBER

OTHER ATTRACTIONS: 2 MILES OF HIKING TRAILS; HISTORIC WOFFORD HOUSE MUSEUM

Fragrant white and blue petunias (left) bloom through spring. The Wofford House (lower left), built in 1850 in Fincastle, Texas, was moved to the Arboretum in 2002 and is now a museum. The dog trot porch courts summer breezes. Coco's House (below) is in the Children's Play Garden.

Next to the lily and koi fish pond is Kathie D. Cox's bronze sculpture of a boy reaching out to a frog (opposite).

THE EL PASO DESERT BOTANICAL GARDEN AT KEYSTONE HERITAGE PARK

The El Paso Desert Botanical Garden stands on 2 acres within the historic Keystone Heritage Park, a site that dates as far back as 4,500 years. Begun in the year 2000 and opened to the public in January 2004, these gardens are entirely the work of volunteers and generous donors—in particular the Junior League of El Paso and the Rotary Club. Individuals and businesses on both sides of the Rio Grande River have contributed to make the El Paso Botanical Garden at Keystone Heritage Park a beautiful place for residents and visitors alike.

In keeping with current concerns about the conservation of natural resources and reducing the carbon footprints of both individuals and institutions, there is a Xeric Demonstration Garden to show how it is possible to have a beautiful garden in a dry climate without wasting water or dosing the plants with chemical fertilizers and pesticides.

In addition, there is a children's garden, an amphitheater for live music and theatrical performances, a moonlight garden, an ethno-botanical timeline garden and a sensory garden with waterfall.

A pit house maze recreates a dwelling like the Native Americans built here during the Archaic period some 4,000 years before the arrival of the Spanish. It has shallow, basin-shaped floors and is covered with an igloo- or tepee-like structure of timber and branches, latilla, plastered over with a thin layer of clay.

A recent addition is the Butterfly House and Butterfly Garden, again planted with native and locally adapted plants that not only take care of the needs of butterflies (also hummingbirds) but have a positive impact on the environment.

Other specialty gardens include an area devoted to cacti and other succulents, a collection of plants used historically for medicinal purposes, and culinary garden of herbs and vegetables.

Finally, for traditionalists, there is a Formal Garden that displays Old World ideas about the art and practice of gardening. Native and locally adapted plants demonstrate how an essentially European-style garden can be quite at home in this arid, mountainous region of the New World.

STANDING STRAIGHT AHEAD FROM THE GARDEN'S MAIN ENTRANCE IS FOUNTAIN PLAZA, WHICH FEATURES A SQUARE POOL WITH A FOUNTAIN IN THE CENTER. AT DUSK, TEMPERATURES DROP AND THE DESERT WINDS DIE DOWN, MAKING IT A POPULAR PLACE FOR EVENING WEDDINGS AND OTHER SPECIAL EVENTS.

ACREAGE: 2 ACRES IN A 52-ACRE PARK

SEASONAL BLOOMS: SPRING, FALL AND AFTER RAIN

OTHER ATTRACTIONS: KEYSTONE HERITAGE PARK'S 4,500-YEAR-OLD SITE INCLUDES ONE OF THE OLDEST VILLAGES IN THE UNITED STATES

NATIVE MOUNTAIN ROCKS EDGE THE WALKWAYS, LINE RAISED PLANTING BEDS AND FORM IMPORTANT WALLS IN THE GARDEN.

TILE MURALS (BELOW) CREATED BY VOLUNTEERS ARE INSET INTO THE WALLS. THIS ONE DEPICTS NATIVE SPECIES OF CACTI.

SCONCE LIGHTS IN ARTS-AND-CRAFTS STYLE (OPPOSITE) FLANK AN ARCH TO THE WALLED GARDENS, WHICH PROTECT PLANTINGS AND VISITORS FROM DAYTIME WINDS AND CREATE A WELCOME SENSE OF ENCLOSURE. OVERHEAD BEAMS EXPRESS AGE-OLD TRADITIONS OF ARBORS AND PERGOLAS AS ESSENTIAL TO THE *Hortus conclusus* OR "ENCLOSED GARDEN."

PLANTS AND FLOWERS IN THE GARDEN OF CACTI AND OTHER SUCCULENTS MERIT CLOSE INSPECTION IN ORDER TO APPRECIATE THEIR OTHER-WORLDLINESS AS COMPARED TO MORE FAMILIAR VARIETIES LIKE ROSES AND GERANIUMS.

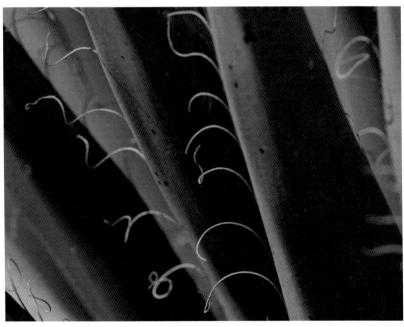

ATTENTION TO UP-CLOSE DETAILS IN THE GARDEN OF CACTI AND OTHER SUCCULENTS REVEALS UNEXPECTED BEAUTY THROUGH A MACRO LENS OR BY THE USE OF A MAGNIFYING GLASS.

THE EL PASO MUNICIPAL ROSE GARDEN

The El Paso Municipal Rose Garden looks like a million dollars, thanks to a recent expansion with a price tag of not quite that, a mere $750,000. The 4-acre garden sits in central El Paso, giving it convenient accessibility to the maximum number of rose admirers. As the name of the garden implies, it is the purview of the City of El Paso Parks and Recreation Department, and the beneficiary of help and advice from the Rose Garden Society and the Texas A&M Extension Service.

The newly enlarged and improved garden took over a year to complete, but the results are such that everyone involved has forgotten the sweat and toil. The garden has outstanding structure, in the form of walls laid of stones from the local mountains. Structure of some type is needed to make rose gardens attractive even when the bushes themselves may not be at their best. Traditionally, this structure has been provided by fiendishly manicured boxwood hedging, which looks beautiful in a formal setting with a be-sheared gardener at the ready to clip the wayward. Here, where Texas ends in the west and, across the Rio Grande River, Mexico begins, such formality could seem out of character if not downright ostentatious.

The multilevel design is compelling in that it lets visitors see the roses from different angles and experience the gardens in their setting in a variety of views. Children love the place for these very reasons, not to mention the waterfalls and the darting koi. A plaza area symbolizes a community place of meeting and is regularly used for weddings, quinceaneras, anniversaries and school graduation celebrations.

More than 4,000 roses grow in the garden, representing the best of all types that are suited to the El Paso growing conditions. Days can be brutally hot through a long summer, but temperatures drop mercifully in the evenings and the winds typical of the daylight hours die down. The most spectacular flowering of the roses occurs in the spring and fall months, in each case after the bushes have been pruned back a bit and given fertilizer.

The citizens of El Paso can take pride in having one of the finest public rose gardens in the country. Not only are the roses remarkable, they also live in beautifully designed architecture built well by proud craftspeople.

AS SURELY AS SPRING MELTS THE MOUNTAIN SNOW CAPS, 'ICEBERG' ROSES FILL THE AIR WITH THEIR HONEY SCENT AND FEATHERY DOUBLE FLOWERS. A FLORIBUNDA, ONE STEM OFTEN HAS ENOUGH BLOOMS TO CONSTITUTE A BOUQUET. EL PASO'S MULTILEVEL MUNICIPAL ROSE GARDEN IS ONE OF THE FINEST IN THE COUNTRY, WITH THE MOST EXUBERANT FLOWERING IN THE SPRING AND AGAIN IN THE FALL.

ACREAGE: 4 ACRES

SEASONAL BLOOMS: SPRING AND FALL, SOME ROSES IN SUMMER

OTHER ATTRACTIONS: WATERFALL, KOI POND AND WALKING PATH

THE WISPY SEEDHEADS OF PRAIRIE Smoke (*Anemone pulsatilla*) FOLLOW THE LAVENDER-BLUE FLOWERS THAT APPEAR AT THE DAWN OF SPRING, SOON AFTER THE ROSES HAVE BEEN PRUNED.

AUTHOR ALICE MORSE EARLE'S CURE FOR A HEADACHE WAS TO PICK A BOUQUET OF ROSES AND PLACE THEM ON HER WRITING TABLE. SOON THE MINGLING FRAGRANCES WORKED THEIR MAGIC AND EARLE (1851-1911) WAS ABLE TO RESUME WORK.

STONES FROM THE NEIGHBORING MOUNTAINS CREATE A DRAMATIC SETTING FOR THE ROSES AND THE MULTILEVELS LET VISITORS EXPERIENCE THE GARDENS FROM MANY ANGLES. COLUMNAR EVERGREENS AND PALM TREES ADD THE VERTICALITY THAT ENERGIZES THE SPACE AND COMPLEMENTS THE ROSES.

RED-AND-WHITE ROSES HAVE BEEN POPULAR SINCE BEFORE 1629 WHEN GARDENERS BEGAN TO GROW THE DAMASK SHRUB ROSE 'YORK AND LANCASTER.' THE SPICY-SCENTED FLORIBUNDA 'SCENTIMENTAL,' A 1997 ALL-AMERICA ROSE SELECTION, BLOOMS OVER A LONG SEASON AND IS ADMIRED BY ALMOST ALL WHO STOOP TO SMELL IT, WOMEN AND MEN ALIKE. TOM CARRUTH, THE BREEDER OF 'SCENTIMENTAL,' SAYS THE STRIPING COMES FROM HERITAGE ROSE GENES.

ASIDE FROM FRAGRANCE, THE TIMELESS APPEAL OF ROSES LIES IN THEIR EXQUISITE FORM AND COLOR, PARTICULARLY THE BLENDED COLORS. 'SEASHELL,' FOR EXAMPLE, HAS BEEN DESCRIBED AS LIKE THE IRIDESCENT COLORS SEEN IN A CONCH SHELL—PEACH, SALMON, PINK, CREAM. THE STALWART 'CARY GRANT' SPORTS LARGE, FULL-PETALED, SPICE-SCENTED FLOWERS IN A BLEND OF ORANGE, COPPER AND GOLD. AND THEN THERE'S THE FRUITY SMELLING SILVERY LILAC-LAVENDER 'BLUE GIRL,' WHICH IN CERTAIN LIGHT AND IN COOLER TIMES OF THE YEAR ALMOST LIVES UP TO THE "BLUE" PART OF ITS NAME. THE LATEST CHALLENGE MET BY ROSE BREEDERS IS TO DEVELOP ROSES WITH PETALS IN FASHIONABLE COLORS, TO MATCH THE LATEST TRENDS IN TEXTILES AND HOME FURNISHINGS.

FORBIDDEN GARDENS

The Forbidden Gardens, a short distance west of Houston, are very, very unique. Built in what was once a rice paddy—yes, Texas does have everything—this re-creation of what has been called the "Eighth Wonder of the World" is marvelous, mysterious, and a little bit creepy. The garden depicts, in one-third scale, the 6,000 life-sized terra-cotta soldiers sculpted to protect the Emperor Qin in his burial chambers three centuries B.C., and unearthed by chance in 1974, 20 miles east of Zi'an, the capital of Shaanxi Province.

Forbidden Gardens, built in 1997, is the creation of a Hong Kong real estate developer, Ira P. H. Poon, who wanted Americans of Asian descent, as well as the public at large, to understand that Asian culture is more than kung-fu, chop suey and fire crackers. Although Poon lives in the Pacific Northwest, he wanted to build his fantasy where it could be outdoors and open all year. Since the Houston metroplex has the third largest Asian population in America, a flat field in Katy, 25 miles to the west, seemed a logical choice.

Largely handcrafted at an estimated cost of $20 million, the Forbidden Gardens cover not only 40 acres but also about 2,000 years of Chinese history. Entry is into a courtyard that seems blessed with tranquility, the air laced with the scent of incense and the haunting sound of a Chinese zither being plucked. A 40,000-square-foot pavilion, open on all sides, shelters awesomely detailed miniature replicas of the Forbidden City of Beijing. And then there is the Emperor Qi's burial ground, with his 6,000 terra-cotta soldiers and horses.

Due to the degrading effects of the intense heat and humidity, some of the painted figures and buildings have experienced bleaching of the paints and buckling of the woods. Because the open-sided Pavilion is oriented north-south, the same as the original Forbidden City, there is no protection from the wind and rain storms that come in from the Gulf of Mexico. Nevertheless, Poon is dedicated to his cause and able to underwrite an estimated $4.5 million restoration of the Forbidden Gardens. That the Forbidden Gardens are a success may be due to the fact that Chinese tourists are flocking to the site, word being that traveling within their own country to see the real thing is more difficult than coming to Katy, Texas.

EMPEROR QIN, SEEN IN THE DISTANCE, OVERLOOKS HIS ARMY OF 6,000 TERRA-COTTA SOLDIERS AND SOME OF THEIR STEEDS, ALL ONE-THIRD-SCALE REPRODUCTIONS AT FORBIDDEN GARDENS. THE FULL-SCALE TERRA-COTTA WARRIORS AND HORSES BURIED WITH THE EMPEROR OVER 2,000 YEARS AGO WERE UNEARTHED IN 1974 NEAR XI'AN BY FARMERS ATTEMPTING TO DIG A WELL FOR WATER.

ACREAGE: 40 ACRES

SEASONAL BLOOMS: NOT APPLICABLE

OTHER ATTRACTIONS: TYWHEELOSAURUS REX IN NEARBY BROOKSHIRE

THE HORSES IN THE FORBIDDEN GARDENS, CREATED AT ONE-THIRD SCALE, SAME AS THE WARRIORS ON CLOSE INSPECTION REVEAL THAT EACH HAS BEEN SCULPTED WITH UNIQUE FEATURES. THE UNEARTHED ORIGINALS DATE BACK OVER 2,000 YEARS AND ARE ESTIMATED TO HAVE BEEN FIRED AT HIGH TEMPERATURES BETWEEN 950 AND 1,050 DEGREES CENTIGRADE, WHICH RESULTED IN MUCH HARDER POTTERY THAN WOULD HAVE BEEN COMMON AT THE TIME. FRAMED BY PINE TREES IN THE DISTANCE AND BLUE PLUMBAGO SHRUBS IN THE FOREGROUND, THE PAVILION EASILY APPEARS TO BE FULL SIZE RATHER THAN A MINIATURE DEPICTION OF A BUILDING IN BEIJING'S FORBIDDEN CITY.

THE ONE-THIRD-SCALE WARRIORS, SOME WITH QUITE PLEASANT EXPRESSIONS, ARE INDIVIDUAL IN DETAIL, FROM BREAST PLATES TO BUCKLES AND HAIR STYLES. BEHIND THEM IS THE FIELD—A FORMER RICE PADDY—OF 6,000 TERRA-COTTA FIGURES AND THE ONE ALMIGHTY EMPEROR QIN.

THE INTRICATE MODEL OF BEIJING'S FORBIDDEN CITY RESIDES UNDER A 40,000-SQUARE-FOOT STEEL CANOPY, TO PROTECT IT FROM THE TEXAS WEATHER. THE HIGHLIGHTS INCLUDE THE GATE OF SUPREME HARMONY, THE PALACE OF HEAVENLY PURITY, THE PALACE OF EARTHLY TRANQUILITY AND THE HALL OF PRESERVING HARMONY. SINCE THE CITY IS MUCH, MUCH SMALLER THAN LIFE, EVEN SCHOOL CHILDREN HAVE FLEETING NOTIONS OF HAVING BECOME TOWERING GIANTS.

MINIATURE FIGURES IN THE RECREATION OF THE FORBIDDEN CITY IN BEIJING—IN REALITY A GATED SANCTUARY OVER 17 MILES LONG—REPRESENT SOLDIERS STANDING GUARD, CONCUBINES GROOMING, EUNUCHS SERVING AND CHILDREN STUDYING.

THE GRAND ENTRANCE TO THE FORBIDDEN GARDENS REVEALS A MYSTERIOUS TABLEAU, MAYBE EVEN A LITTLE FRIGHTENING TO A SMALL CHILD UNACCUSTOMED TO SEEING HORSES AND CHARIOT FOLLOWED BY FEARSOME LOOKING CHINESE WARRIORS. LIKE THE TERRA-COTTA WARRIORS, THE HORSES' HEADS AND BODIES ARE HOLLOW, THE LEGS SOLID. IT IS BELIEVED THAT THE BODY PARTS WERE MADE IN SEPARATE MOLDS FROM LOCAL CLAY, THEN ASSEMBLED AND GLUED TOGETHER BEFORE FIRING THE POTTERY. THE BASIC PARTS WERE PROBABLY CAST BY THE SAME WORKERS WHO NORMALLY PRODUCED CLAY DRAIN TILES AND THE FACIAL FEATURES SUCH AS EYES, EARS, NOSE AND HAIR WERE INDIVIDUALLY SCULPTED BEFORE FIRING. THE ORIGINAL WARRIORS VARIED IN HEIGHT FROM 6 TO 6.5 FEET, THE TALLER BEING THE GENERALS; THE HORSES WERE COMMENSURATE IN SIZE.

THE FORT WORTH BOTANIC GARDENS

The creators of the Fort Worth Botanic Garden had to be brave and courageous and maybe a little reckless to have launched such a project in the midst of the Great Depression, but because they did, succeeding generations can boast with impugnity that theirs is the oldest such institution in Texas. For comparison, the Missouri Botanic Garden in St. Louis, one of the oldest in America, was founded as Shaw's Garden in 1859, and the Chicago Botanic Garden not until 1972. The world's oldest botanical garden, dating from 1544, is alive and well today in Padua, Italy.

An early beginning has assured the Fort Worth Botanic Garden a site that is in the heart of Fort Worth's Cultural District. To have over a hundred acres vegetated by some 2,500 species of native and exotic plants in 23 specialty gardens in an urban setting is highly unusual, if not priceless, in terms of accessibility. Modest fees are charged to enter the conservatory and Japanese garden; otherwise, admission is free.

The design of the Lower Rose Garden was inspired by Italy's Villa Lante, considered one of the finest gardens ever created. Although there are rose blossoms almost any day from Easter to Thanksgiving and sometimes Christmas, the roses mostly go all to bloom in the spring and again in the fall, after they recover from the intense summer heat. The best of Texas-acclimated roses populate the Oval Rose Garden.

In keeping with its mission, to enrich lives through environmental stewardship and education, the Fort Worth Botanic Garden has added a Water Wise Entrance at the northern gateway to the Garden. Here are featured colorful native plants that use little water and put on a colorful show from April through October. The Texas Native Forest Boardwalk lets visitors get up close to trees in a way not possible looking from the ground up. A Trial Garden lets visitors be on the inside track in evaluating which new varieties of perennials will make the grade and be added to permanent plantings.

The Conservatory, with its 10,000 square feet for growing tropicals, is a favorite winter destination. Besides towering palms and other exotic trees, there are orchids, bromeliads and foliage plants in a colorful tapestry.

A Four Seasons Garden is lined with beds of hundreds of different iris, daylilies and chrysanthemums deftly planted in sunny places between the live oaks that shade benches and make this a favorite spot for visitors to take it easy.

FORT WORTH ARTIST EVALINE CLARKE SELLORS (1903-1995) SCULPTED THE TEXAS-SIZE STONEWARE FROG THAT IS PERPETUALLY ABOUT TO LEAP INTO THE POOL AND FOUNTAIN IN THE FRAGRANCE GARDEN. PLANTS HAVING SCENTED LEAVES AND FRAGRANT FLOWERS ARE FEATURED IN THIS "SANCTUARY FOR THE SENSES," WHICH IS A FAVORITE PLACE FOR SMALL WEDDINGS AND GARDEN PARTIES.

ACREAGE: 109 ACRES

SEASONAL BLOOMS: AMONG THE 150,000 PLANTS, SOMETHING IS ALWAYS OF INTEREST

OTHER ATTRACTIONS: RESTAURANT AND RENTALS FOR SPECIAL EVENTS

THE TEA HOUSE (ABOVE) OVER-LOOKS THE 7-ACRE JAPANESE GARDEN WITH WATERFALLS, A MEDITATION SPACE AND PONDS THAT ARE HOME TO COLORFUL KOI. A MULTILEVEL JAPANESE LANTERN (RIGHT) STANDS BEHIND TEXAS WISTERIA; ITS FRAGRANT FLOWERS APPEAR IN THE SPRING AFTER IT HAS LEAFED OUT. KNOWN BOTANICALLY AS *Wisteria frutescens*, IT IS LESS AGGRESSIVE THAN ASIAN WISTERIAS.

EACH SEASON FRAMES THE ELEGANT MOON BRIDGE WITH BEAUTY: IN EARLY SPRING THERE ARE AZALEAS AND FLOWERING TREES; SUMMER IS A MEDLEY OF GREENS; FALL FEATURES JAPANESE MAPLES IN RIOTOUS RED AND GOLD; WINTER PLAYS UP THE PINE TREES—AND ON OCCASION A BLANKET OF SNOW CREATES A SERENE WONDERLAND.

A Japanese flowering cherry tree (above) makes a breath-taking sight in spring and in winter the bare branches reveal the exquisite silvery ruby-colored bark.

Towering trees (opposite, upper left) give shelter to Japanese cut-leaf maples and other under-story trees. The wheelchair-accessible boardwalk invites everyone to explore.

Stone, earth, leaf and water (opposite, lower left) are said to become one in the Japanese garden. A sculpture of water fowl that appear to be either landing or about to take off centers one of numerous ponds that attract real birds and other wildlife. The golden yellow Japanese rose (*Kerria japonica 'Pleniflora'*) blooms in the foreground.

HERMANN PARK

New York has Central Park (843 acres), Chicago has Garfield (185 acres), Los Angeles has Griffith (100 acres), San Francisco has Golden Gate Park (1017 acres). And then there's Hermann Park, 445 green acres south of Houston's original downtown. As big city parks go, Hermann ranks as one of the best for the variety and quality of its attractions—zoo, aquarium, natural science museum, planetarium, butterfly center, Japanese garden, rose garden, live theater and music, golf, train rides—while at the same time providing restorative green space at the heart of a metropolis.

Hermann Park began in 1914 when the Board of Parks Commissioner, one George Hermann, donated the 285 acres with which to begin. He died later that year and in 1915 the city purchased additional acreage to complete the park. As a young man, Hermann operated a saw mill on this site, which earned him money to invest in real estate, and the discovery in 1903 of oil on a property he owned in Humble made him a millionaire, and a most generous one. Recent improvements in the heart of the park, led by landscape architect Laurie Olin, have earned it an Award of Excellence from the American Society of Landscape Architects.

The formalized gardens within Hermann Park are of particular note here—the Houston Garden center, an inviting place for garden club meetings; the International Sculpture Garden with its signature monument to Dr. Mahatma Gandhi; and the Japanese Garden by Japanese landscape architect Ken Nakajima, who based his design on the Zen belief that, "We must work with nature, to create a new space and a sense of beauty."

The outdoor spaces surrounding the Garden Center abound with roses, many of them old-fashioned, along with culinary and medicinal herbs and perennial flowers arranged according to Western ideas about garden design. The Japanese garden, with its elegant teahouse, built in Japan and reconstructed here by Japanese craftsmen, as well as waterfalls and stone lanterns, demonstrates Eastern ideas about landscaping.

Houston's freeways and the expanding Metro Rail make Hermann Park accessible to everyone—for an hour of stress relief, a day of fun and picnicking, or a week if you want to take in all the attractions, many of which are free. The park itself is bounded by the Museum District, Rice University and the Medical Center, literally the heart—and some would say the lungs—of the city.

GENERAL SAM HOUSTON, ONE OF THE CITY'S FOUNDERS, IN A BRONZE LIKENESS ON HIS MIGHTY STEED, OVERSEES THE MAIN NORTH ENTRANCE TO HERMANN PARK, AT THE INTERSECTION OF MAIN STREET AND MONTROSE BOULEVARD. FLOWERY BORDERS FEATURE CREAMY WHITE LANTANA, BLUE SAGE AND PINK LANDSCAPE ROSES.

ACREAGE: 445 ACRES

SEASONAL BLOOMS: LATE WINTER/SPRING: AZALEAS, MAGNOLIAS, ROSES; SUMMER: CRAPE MYRTLES, GINGERS, HIBISCUS; FALL: ROSES

OTHER ATTRACTIONS: PICNICKING AND PLAYGROUNDS, HIKING AND BIKING, PUBLIC GOLD COURSE, BIRD AND WETLAND HABITAT, MINIATURE TRAIN TRACK

A monument to Dr. Mahatma Gandhi (near right) stands in a reflecting pool among fountains in the International Sculpture Garden next to the Houston Garden Center. Spring plantings feature pink geraniums, silver dusty miller and purple petunias. Orange-red nasturtiums and golden pineapple sage with red flowers (opposite, left) bloom at the Garden Center. The many roses include 'Carefree Delight' (opposite, far right).

THIS PART OF HERMANN PARK IS CULTIVATED TO LOOK A LITTLE WILD, TO OFFER THE ALLURE OF TAKING A STROLL TO EXPLORE THE WOODLAND. AZALEAS COLOR THE SCENE IN EARLY SPRING, FOLLOWED BY LOUISIANA IRIS, WHICH LIKE THEIR ROOTS IN OR NEAR WATER AT THE BEGINNING OF THE GROWING SEASON.

The Japanese garden and tea-house is one of the jewels in Hermann Park, a place that by nature invites contemplation. Every tree, shrub and rock was chosen to fulfill the vision of the designer, Ken Nakajima. Even in sultry weather the water and muted colors are calming and cooling to the senses.

THE SLAT HOUSE SHADE STRUCTURE AT THE HOUSTON GARDEN CENTER IN HERMANN PARK IS CENTERED BY A TIERED FOUNTAIN THAT MASKS URBAN NOISE WHILE OFFERING ACCOMPANIMENT TO THE RESIDENT BIRDS. RAISED PLANTING BEDS SPILL OVER WITH ORANGE AND GOLD NASTURTIUMS AND THE BLUE OF BORAGE AND LAVENDER. THE TALL STEMS WITH WHORLS OF ORANGE FLOWERS BELONG TO LION'S TAIL (*Leonotis leonurus*).

HOUSTON ARBORETUM AND NATURE CENTER

It is common knowledge that some seeds will not germinate unless passed through the digestive system of an animal or until they have been subjected to fire or alternate freezing and thawing. More often than not, public gardens share a similar path of trial and tribulation before the seeds of ideas planted by the founders come to fruition. The Houston Arboretum is a good case in point. Robert A. Vines, an ecologist and educator, first proposed the idea of carving out a piece of land from Memorial Park, one of the largest in the nation, to serve as a nature sanctuary around 1950. In 1951 the City Council agreed with him and set aside 265 acres that, through dint of road building and rights-of-way, would be reduced to the present 155. Ground for a nature center building was not broken until 1967 and it would be 1995 before the state-of-the-art Discovery Room exhibits could be added. As predicted, this improvement acted like fertilizer on the growth of the institution.

The Meadow Restoration Project began in 1999 and through the cooperation of numerous state and local agencies, the Arboretum performed a long-needed prescribed burn to re-energize the soil and improve the meadow's vegetation. In the fall of 2000 the Charlotte Couch Memorial Birding Walkway was dedicated, employing a raised boardwalk that lets visitors enjoy views of Buffalo Bayou and the forest canopy without impacting the fragile ecosystem. Without the raised and defined walkways, a single clump of colorful wildflowers could draw hundreds of admirers trampling over anything in their path toward seeing the flower up close and maybe snapping a picture.

A Wildlife Garden has lately been installed, to demonstrate plantings suited to urban backyards for attracting hummingbirds, butterflies and other wildlife. Visitors learn the necessity of providing food, shelter, water and space for wildlife like that observed at the Arboretum—five-lined skink, the State Bird of Texas (Northern mockingbird), swamp rabbit and the nine-banded armadillo.

Another recent addition is the Carol Tatkon Sensory Garden, which showcases native plants that nurture the senses—scented leaves, fragrant flowers, color, touch and sound. For example, the parsley hawthorn (*Crataegus marshallii*) is covered by tiny white fragrant blooms in spring, red berries in the fall, and flaking gray bark that reveals orange in the layer underneath. Coral honeysuckle (*Lonicera sempervirens*) has blue-green foliage year round and coral-red flowers the hummingbirds love to visit.

ACREAGE: 155 ACRES

SEASONAL BLOOMS: PRIMARILY LATE-WINTER/SPRING AND FALL

OTHER ATTRACTIONS: DISCOVERY ROOMS WITH INTERACTIVE EXHIBITS; AQUARIUM

WATER LILIES NOT YET IN BLOOM SHARE THE POND WITH WATER SNOWFLAKE (*Nymphoides indica*), WHICH PRODUCES COUNTLESS SMALL WHITE FLOWERS HAVING FRINGED PETALS AND WHICH STAND UP ABOVE THE SURFACE THE SAME AS TROPICAL WATER LILIES. NATIVE PINES AND OAKS GROW IN THE BACKGROUND.

LOUISIANA IRIS HAVE NATURALIZED
ALONG THE BANKS OF THE POND.
WHILE THEY MAY APPEAR DELICATE,
THE PLANTS ARE STRONG AND
RETURN YEARLY IN INCREASING
NUMBERS.

A LAVENDER-BLUE GULF COAST
PENSTEMON, ALSO CALLED BRAZOS
PENSTEMON, MAKES AN EXCELLENT
COMPANION FOR AN OLD ROSE.
BOTH ARE SURVIVORS IN THE
HOUSTON AREA.

GOOSENECK PLANTS AND LOUISIANA IRIS HAVE COLONIZED THE BANKS OF A POND. IN THE EVENT OF A DROUGHT, THEY'LL DIE BACK BUT MAKE A STRONG RETURN FOLLOWING RAIN. IT IS THE GOAL OF THE ARBORETUM TO LET NATURE BE NATURE AND NOT TO IMPOSE THE CONTROL EVIDENCED IN FORMAL CULTIVATED GARDENS.

HUGH RAMSEY NATURE PARK

A gateway to the World Birding Center, Harlingen's Hugh Ramsey Nature Park is a shining example of a wondrous thing wrought when public services and private organizations join together in achieving a common goal. Up until 1992 these 50-some-odd acres had been a landfill, then they were declared park space and work began— thousands of hours of work by city employees and volunteers, in particular members of the Arroyo Colorado Audubon Society and the Texas Master Naturalists.

After clearing the land of invasive exotic species and opening up walking trails, native trees and shrubs were transplanted to the site. These include Texas ebony (*Pithecellobium flexicaule*), huisache (*Acacia farnesiana*), retama or Jerusalem thorn (*Parkinsonia aculeata*), honey mesquite (*Prosopis glandulosa*) and granjeno or spiny hackberry (*Celtis Ilida*)—all chosen because they are self-reliant in the local conditions and provide protective habitat for birds and other wildlife.

A garden of plants that attract and serve the life-cycle needs of butterflies is cultivated next to the parking lot and serves as the entry point to walking trails and open areas for observing the wildlife. The Ebony Trail represents the beginnings of a botanic garden and leads to a collection of medicinal plants and other specialty gardens dedicated to individuals having a passion for a particular kind of plant or type of garden.

While it is convenient to major highways and an international airport, the Harlingen Arroyo Colorado area continues to be a quiet woodland retreat and a gateway to the World Birding Center network. This increasingly precious reservoir of nature is connected by the arroyo waterway and hiking and biking trails through the city of Harlingen, with Hugh Ramsey Nature Park on the east side and the Harlingen Thicket on the west.

Ramsey's 55 acres of Texas ebony woodlands and the Thicket's 40 acres of upland thorn forest represent a conservationist's dream by providing refuge for birds and a host of other creatures in what is essentially the heart of an urban center. While city employees act as facilitators, they are quick to say that volunteers do most of the work. Whether tree, shrub, groundcover or flowering plant, the guiding rule is that it be native or locally adapted, not invasive, and not require irrigation other than possibly when newly planted.

The Ramsey and the Thicket are breeding grounds for birds including Valley specialties—the Green and Ringed Kingfishers, Common Pauraque, Groove-billed Ani, Long-billed Thrasher and Olive Sparrow. At times of migration, the endangered Red-crown Parrots, also stop for a rest and food.

HUMMINGBIRDS ARE AMONG VISITORS' FAVORITE ATTRACTIONS AT HUGH RAMSEY NATURE PARK. BENCHES ARE STRATEGICALLY PLACED SO THAT BIRDERS MAY SIT QUIETLY AND OBSERVE WITHOUT DISTURBING THE HUMMINGBIRDS AS THEY FEED, BUILD NESTS AND NURTURE THEIR YOUNG.

ACREAGE: 55 ACRES

SEASONAL BLOOMS: FLOWERS AND BIRDS IN ALL SEASONS

OTHER ATTRACTIONS: NATURE TRAILS. WEDNESDAYS IN SUMMER, VISIT ARROYO COLORADO AUDUBON SOCIETY GROUP MEETINGS

A FEMALE HUMMINGBIRD (LEFT) ALIGHTS ON THE NEST SHE BUILT WITH HER MATE IN THE BRANCHES OF A HUISACHE OR ACACIA TREE. THE OPENED SEEDPOD OF THE TREE, ABOUT THE SIZE OF A LIMA BEAN POD, ALMOST DWARFS THE BIRD.

NATIVE CACTI SUCH AS THE PRICKLY PEAR (OPPOSITE) GROW IN OPEN, SUNNY PLACES AND BLOOM SOON AFTER A RAIN.

THE LADY BIRD JOHNSON WILDFLOWER CENTER

Lady Bird Johnson will never be forgotten—for a variety of reasons—but she will likely be most remembered for her efforts to make America more beautiful. It was she who dared in the 1960s to speak out about the ugliness of unfettered development and the litter on highway roadsides. In her gentle way, she taught us that the world would be a better place if everyone just planted a tree, a shrub or some flowers and, for heaven's sake, got in the habit of picking up litter.

Many of us eagerly joined Lady Bird's crusade. The record shows about half the world's botanic gardens have been created since 1950, and that doesn't include the myriad public gardens not cataloged literally as "botanic gardens," among them Lady Bird's own National Wildflower Research Center, which she founded in 1982—at the age of 70—with actress and gardener Helen Hayes.

The Center's first home was a small house on a plot of undeveloped land east of Austin. Lady Bird furnished it with a genius plantsman, garden designer and communicator, Dr. Carleton B. Lees. As Dr. Lees got to work laying the groundwork, Lady Bird herself made sure he had the necessities for making the place both his home and office.

In 1983 the Junior League of Austin pledged to give $30,000 over a three-year period to develop a volunteer program. The Center's first research project was begun in 1984, the same year Lady Bird received a Congressional Gold Medal for her dedication to the beautification of America. The lavishly illustrated *Wildflowers Across America*, by Lady Bird and Dr. Lees, was published in 1988, and the Jubilee Celebration held in Washington, D.C., honoring Lady Bird's 75th birthday raised more than a million dollars for the work of the Center.

The 1995 opening of a new facility on 43 acres at the present site was followed by its renaming in 1997 as the Lady Bird Johnson Wildflower Center and the establishment of the Brown Center for Environmental Education. Since then, a total of 236 adjacent acres have been added, bringing the total to 279 acres.

It has been said the best mission statements are those that become part of us and the Wildflower Center's is a model of simplicity: "To increase the sustainable use and conservation of native wildflowers, plants and landscapes." Hardly anything could be nicer than a visit to the Lady Bird Johnson Wildflower Center, but until you are able to do so, watch for evidence of the seeds she planted to beautify all of America.

ALL PLANTS, TREES AND SHRUBS AT THE LADY BIRD JOHNSON WILDFLOWER CENTER ARE TEXAS NATIVES. PURPLE CONEFLOWERS (*Echinacea purpurea*) BLOOM IN THIS PHOTOGRAPH TAKEN IN THE EARLY SPRING. THE CENTER'S NEW FACILITIES OPENED IN 1995 AS A MODEL OF "TOTAL RESOURCE CONSERVATION" AND SUBSEQUENTLY HAVE RECEIVED NUMEROUS ENVIRONMENTAL AND ARCHITECTURAL AWARDS.

ACREAGE: 279 ACRES

SEASONAL BLOOMS: PRIMARILY EARLY SPRING THROUGH EARLY SUMMER AND AGAIN IN FALL, DEPENDING ON RAINFALL

OTHER ATTRACTIONS: THE WILDFLOWER CENTER IS AN OFFICIAL COMPONENT OF THE UNIVERSITY OF TEXAS AT AUSTIN, AS AN ORGANIZED RESEARCH UNIT OF THE COLLEGE OF NATURAL SCIENCES AND THE SCHOOL OF ARCHITECTURE

THE COURTYARD OF THE WILDFLOWER CENTER DEFINES OASIS WITH ITS WATER, GREEN NATIVE VEGETATION AND SHELTERING WALLS OF LOCAL STONE.

IN 1988 WHEN THE NATIONAL WILDFLOWER RESEARCH CENTER CHANGED ITS NAME TO HONOR ITS FOUNDER, LADY BIRD WAS JOINED BY LAURA BUSH, THEN FIRST LADY OF TEXAS, AT THE RE-DEDICATION CEREMONY.

A FIELD OF BLUEBONNETS (*Lupinus subcarnosus*), THE TEXAS STATE FLOWER, BLOOMS IN EARLY SPRING AT THE WILDFLOWER CENTER, PUNCTUATED BY STANDS OF GLOWING YELLOW-FLOWERED PRICKLY PEAR CACTI. BOTH PLANTS THRIVE ON POOR SOIL. AUSTIN HAS AN AVERAGE ANNUAL RAINFALL OF 32 INCHES. THE DRIEST MONTHS ARE JANUARY-MARCH, THE WETTEST APRIL-JUNE, WHEN THE BLUEBONNETS BLOOM AND SEPTEMBER-OCTOBER, WHEN THE NEXT YEAR'S BLUEBONNET SEEDLINGS ARE TAKING ROOT.

LUBBOCK MEMORIAL ARBORETUM

The founders of the Lubbock Memorial Arboretum saw it as a museum of living plants, with emphasis on trees that could survive and maybe even thrive in the often harsh climate. Those who carry the torch today also see it as a place to showcase shrubs, vines, perennials and ornamental grasses adapted to the area, a laboratory for experimenting with new plants.

The Arboretum began as a project of the Lubbock Council of Garden Clubs, some members of which also served on the Garden-Arts Center Board that worked with the City of Lubbock Parks Planning Board and Board of City Commissioners in developing the Garden-Arts Center in K.N. Clapp Park. Robert H. Rucker, a professor of horticulture, was commissioned to develop a plan for an arboretum, which was approved in 1961, to include the 94 acres of park land in K.N. Clapp Park that were not designated recreation areas. Rucker proposed five feature gardens. He envisioned plants that would range from indigenous to exotic.

Actual planting got underway on Arbor Day, January 19, 1962, when spades sliced through the earth and made a place for a Western Schley pecan in front of the Garden and Arts Center. The J.A. Hodges Rose Garden was planted with 150 rosebushes in the spring of 1963.

The Tea Terrace which extends from the southeast corner of the Garden and Arts Center, was donated by the Lubbock Council of Garden Clubs in 1967. The next year a large oak planting was underwritten by the Lubbock Rose Society, Kentucky coffee trees by a local landscaper and wrought-iron fencing for the Japanese garden was added to secure the stone lanterns. A formal Fragrance Garden followed in 1969, also a gift of the Lubbock Garden Club.

Over the years, many hundreds of trees have been planted, as memorials and to honor individuals who have made contributions to the cultural life of Lubbock. A Western planting initiated in 1980 stressed planting only plants found native within 150 miles of the city.

The opening of the Arboretum Interpretive Center in 1992 greatly enhanced the institution's ability to offer educational programs. Perhaps most remarkable about the Arboretum is that everything has been accomplished by volunteers. A part-time office manager was the first paid employee in 1997. The Georgia Williams Green and White Garden is the setting for the St. Paul's-on-the-Plains Historic Episcopal Church. The Church, the oldest public building in Lubbock, was moved from its original location at 16th and Avenue O, to the Arboretum in 1997.

WITH OR WITHOUT SEASONAL FLOWERS, THE ARBORETUM IS A TRANQUIL SETTING WITH ORDERED WALKWAYS, PATHS AND RESTING PLACES FOR CONTEMPLATING THE VISTAS. EARLY MORNINGS AND LATE AFTERNOONS FAVOR THE MOST FLATTERING LIGHT FOR VIEWING THE INTENSE COLORS OF FLOWERS AND APPRECIATING THE MANY DIFFERENT TEXTURES.

ACREAGE: 94 ACRES

SEASONAL BLOOMS: Spring: flowering trees, shrubs, bulbs, peonies, iris; Summer: roses and annuals; Fall: chrysanthemums

OTHER ATTRACTIONS: Visual and performing arts in K.N. Clapp Park

TALL BEARDED IRIS (CLOCKWISE, FROM TOP LEFT) MAKE A RAINBOW OF COLOR IN MAY. CALIFORNIA POPPIES SELF-SOW AND BLOOM IN DELIGHTFULLY UNEXPECTED PLACES. BRIDAL-WREATH SPIREA IS LIKE SNOW IN LATE SPRING. FRUITS OF THE CHINABERRY TREE GLOW IN THE WARM LIGHT OF SUNRISE.

THE LOUTHAN JAPANESE GARDEN, SITUATED BEHIND THE GARDEN AND ARTS CENTER, WAS DEDICATED IN 1964. THE TEA TERRACE THAT EXTENDS FROM THE SOUTHEAST CORNER OF THE CENTER REPRESENTS VARIOUS TYPES OF MATERIAL THAT CAN BE USED FOR PATIOS AND GARDEN WALKS.

TALL BEARDED OR GERMAN IRIS THRIVE IN THE LUBBOCK CLIMATE, WHICH GIVES THEM THE MOISTURE THEY NEED IN SPRING THROUGH THE BLOOMING SEASON, THEN TURNS DRY WHEN THEY NEED A TIME OF REST. THE DWARF TYPES BLOOM FIRST, USUALLY IN APRIL, FOLLOWED BY THE BIG ONES.

MERCER ARBORETUM

Located immediately northeast of Houston's George Bush Intercontinental Airport, the improbably named city of Humble is home to Mercer Arboretum and Botanic Gardens, a spectacular place filled with gardens and nature trails that welcomes over a quarter million visitors each year. Admission is free. There is hardly a time not to visit—the 20 acres of cultivated gardens alone are packed with plants of interest in all seasons.

Mercer is named for Thelma and Charles Mercer, a couple of modest means who purchased 14.5 acres of East Texas piney woods in 1949 and set about selectively clearing the land and planting gardens. Upon retirement in 1973, the Mercers struck a deal with Harris County: They would sell the property at a bargain price in return for its being turned into a public garden with a strong emphasis on education. Over the years additional parcels of land have been purchased, until today the total stands at about 300 acres. The cultivated, educational components are located on the east side of Aldine Westfield Road, while on the west side there are woodlands, picnic areas, two barbecue pavilions, a cypress swamp and miles of trails and boardwalks.

The "arboretum" part of Mercer's name refers to the vast collection of woody plants—trees and shrubs; "botanic gardens" refers to plantings devoted variously to butterfly plants, seasonal displays, herbs, a maze, Texas native plants, perennials, roses and tropicals. There are also specialty plant collections featuring gingers, ferns, bamboo, Louisiana iris and daylilies. Gardeners in Greater Houston are inclined to taking a gamble on whether or not a new plant can take the decidedly tropical summers but also survive the occasional deep freeze. Thelma Mercer herself set the example by introducing to these parts the prehistoric ginkgo tree (her original plantings have now naturalized), bauhinia with its orchid-like flowers and philadelphus or mock-orange.

Mercer is one of 36 premier botanical gardens and arboretums that help maintain the National Collection of Endangered Plants for the Center of Plant Conservation. On display in the Endangered Species Garden are 24 rare plants that Mercer shelters.

March Mart, Mercer's annual spring plant sale, brings gardening enthusiasts in droves, some no doubt looking for bargains, most in search of something new to challenge horticultural skills and possibly to impress the neighbors. The staff botanists, horticulturists and gardeners quietly educate by introducing to the sale new or different plants they admire but that amateurs might not know.

AS A MAGNET FOR CHILDREN, HARDLY ANYTHING MATCHES A NATURAL POND WITH FROLICKING GOLDFISH AND STEPPING STONES THAT INVITE CROSSINGS AND MAYBE GETTING A LITTLE WET. A SHADED BENCH AND LUSH PLANTINGS ALSO MAKE THIS AN IDYLLIC SETTING FOR A SERENE ENCOUNTER WITH NATURE. A CUT-LEAF JAPANESE MAPLE CAN BE SEEN IN THE FOREGROUND AND BEHIND IT ARE THE BOLD ROUND LEAVES OF LEOPARD PLANT. FERNS HAVE TAKEN ROOT BETWEEN THE STONES.

ACREAGE: 300+ ACRES

SEASONAL BLOOMS: Something in bloom 365 days

OTHER ATTRACTIONS: Picnic grounds, hiking trails, barbecue pavilions, boardwalks to explore the cypress swamp

Buddha's belly bamboo (*Bambusa tuldoides 'Ventricosa'*) grows in clumps to 40 feet tall, with evergreen leaves. While prone to invasiveness, in the right place this can be a magnificent specimen, one tough enough to weather the occasional hurricane. In everyday breezes, the rubbing together of the canes—technically the culms—makes a creaking sound reminiscent of a ship at sea.

THE CLUMP-FORMING PAINTED BAMBOO OR GOLDEN HAWAIIAN BAMBOO (*Bambusa vulgaris* 'Striata'—FOR THE GREEN STRIPES, AND SOMETIMES AS 'Vittata') CAN GROW TO 50 FEET TALL WITH INDIVIDUAL CANES TO 4 INCHES IN DIAMETER. THERE IS NOTHING SUBTLE ABOUT THIS GIANT, IT IS QUITE SIMPLY STUNNING. FIRST DESCRIBED AROUND 1800 IN HEIDELBURG, GERMANY, THE VARIETY IS ANCIENT IN CULTIVATION THROUGHOUT CENTRAL AMERICA AND HAWAII. PAINTED BAMBOO IS SO STRIKINGLY ORNAMENTAL, IT IS ALMOST UNTHINKABLE THAT IN THE PHILIPPINES THE CANES ARE USED FOR PRODUCING PAPER PULP.

A TROPICAL WATER LILY (UPPER LEFT) IS A MAGICAL THING TO WATCH UNFOLD IN THE MORNING SUN, TO BECOME A STARRY FLOWER THE SIZE OF A SAUCER. MERCER'S COLLECTION INCLUDES MANY COLORS AND BLOOMS FROM LATE SPRING TO EARLY FALL. AS DISTINGUISHED FROM THE HARDY TYPES, WHOSE FLOWERS FLOAT ON THE WATER, TROPICAL WATER LILIES STAND ON STEMS THAT RISE REGALLY ABOVE THE SURFACE.

THE PHAIUS OR NUN ORCHID IS A TERRESTRIAL SPECIES FROM ASIA THAT THRIVES OUTDOORS ALL YEAR WHERE WINTER IS UNLIKELY TO BRING PROTRACTED DEEP FREEZES. IT HAS ATTRACTIVE PLEATED FOLIAGE ABOVE WHICH THE FLOWER SPIKES CAN GROW TO 4 FEET TALL IN SPRING AND SUMMER. PHAIUS ARE INCREASINGLY GROWN IN SHADE GARDENS THROUGHOUT THE DEEP SOUTH AND SOME HAVE EVEN NATURALIZED IN FLORIDA WETLANDS.

TEXAS NATIVES AND LOCALLY ADAPTED EXOTICS THAT DON'T REQUIRE UNDUE IRRIGATION DURING NORMAL PERIODS OF DROUGHT THRIVE IN THIS INVITING GARDEN AT MERCER. THE BUBBLING FOUNTAINS SOOTHE THE SENSES WHILE THE RAISED BEDS EASE THE GARDENERS' WORK AND PROVIDE A PLACE FOR VISITORS TO SIT A SPELL AND SOAK UP THE SOUNDS AND THE BEAUTY. THE RED FLOWERS AND FERNY FOLIAGE BEHIND THE MAIN FOUNTAIN BELONG TO *Russellia equisetiformis*, A MEXICAN RELATIVE OF THE SNAPDRAGON THAT IS IN FREQUENT BLOOM.

MOODY GARDENS

There is no place in the world quite like Moody Gardens, a tourist complex owned by the City of Galveston that is operated and supported by the vastly deep-pocketed Moody Foundation. Considering that it began in the mid-1980s with a horse barn and arena, its present-day claim as "one of the premier educational/recreational facilities in the Southwest" may be judged a model of understatement.

From the outset, Moody Gardens' founders aimed high. They sought guidance from one of the 20th century's most visionary architects, Sir Geoffrey Jellicoe (1900-1999) of the United Kingdom. The initial purpose, to begin a hippotherapy riding program for people with head injuries, still informs the Gardens' horticultural therapy programs, education and employment of persons with a wide range of physical and emotional disabilities.

Apart from the lavishly landscaped grounds, the Rainforest Pyramid and IMAX 3D Theater Complex draw hundreds of thousands of visitors annually, who heap praises on the experience. The Rainforest Pyramid is quite simply awesome from the outside and, once inside, everyday reality fades in the face of more than 1,700 exotic and animal species from the rainforests of Asia, the tropical Americas and Africa.

Inside the Rainforest Pyramid there are three distinct geographical regions to explore: Asia, Africa and America. Within each are plants, animals, fish and birds native to each. As a member of the American Zoo and Aquarium Association, Moody Gardens works to ensure long-term survival of captive wildlife populations including the Pink Pigeon, Ocelot, Cotton-Top Tamarin, Pygmy Slow Loris and Tomato Frog.

The American rainforest, which stretches from southern Mexico through Central America, the Caribbean islands and into South America, is the largest and most biologically diverse. The more than 25,000 plants endemic to this region include those used for medicine by native populations as well as a host of species that are familiar as houseplants and in tropical gardens, such as members of the philodendron, orchid, pineapple, fern and gesneriad families.

The Asian rainforest, besides the tropical forests in Asia, include those of Australia and the Pacific Islands. The epiphytes or air plants include certain aroids or members of the philodendron family, an astounding array of orchids and enormous bird's-nest and staghorn ferns.

The African rainforest often comes as a surprise to visitors since news from this continent so often has to do with horrendous drought and famine. Nevertheless, there are places with the necessary moisture to grow ficus, mahogany and ebony trees, certain orchids and the popular African violet, discovered in 1892 by Baron Walter von St. Paul in East Africa.

THE GLASS-ENCLOSED RAINFOREST PYRAMID IS 10 STORIES HIGH AND IS DESIGNED TO WITHSTAND HURRICANE-FORCE WINDS, A MAJOR CONSIDERATION FOR GALVESTON, A CITY THAT WAS DESTROYED BY THE HURRICANE OF 1900. INSIDE THE PYRAMID ARE 1,700 PLANT AND ANIMAL SPECIES FROM THE RAIN-FORESTS OF ASIA, THE TROPICAL AMERICAS AND AFRICA.

ACREAGE: 142 ACRES

SEASONAL BLOOMS: ALL YEAR, INSIDE AND OUT

OTHER ATTRACTIONS: AQUARIUM PYRAMID; DISCOVERY PYRAMID; HOTEL AND CONVEN-TION CENTER; WHITE FLORIDA SAND BEACH

MOODY GARDENS' PALM BEACH FEATURES TONS OF WHITE FLORIDA SAND HAULED BY BARGE ACROSS THE GULF OF MEXICO, TO CREATE A PLACE FOR FAMILY PLAY. THE LAND-SCAPING IN GRAND CURVING BEDS WITH EXPOSED AGGREGATE PAVING IS ACCESSIBLE TO ALL, INCLUDING WHEELCHAIRS AND STROLLERS. THE PLANTINGS ARE DEVOTED TO NATIVE AND LOCALLY ADAPTED EXOTICS, INCLUDING THE FLAM-BOYANTLY COLORED HAWAIIAN TI PLANT (*cordyline*), FIREBUSH (*Hamelia patens*, A BUTTERFLY AND HUMMINGBIRD MAGNET) AND THE EVERBLOOMING FIRECRACKER PLANT (*Russellia equisetiformis*).

THE ANNUAL HOLIDAY FESTIVAL OF
LIGHTS DRAWS LARGE CROWDS—A
POPULAR EVENT FOR BOTH VISITORS
AND LOCAL GALVESTONIANS.
THE GARDEN PATHS BECOME A
WONDERLAND OF DELIGHTS FOR
CHILDREN OF ALL AGES.

Soaring palms and ficus trees in a setting of natural streams and faux but real-looking boulders obscure the reality of the space in the Pyramid. Bromeliads, orchids and rainforest cacti perch on apparently fallen tree branches, the same as they do in nature.

Bromeliads (opposite page, clockwise from upper left), ornamental relatives of the pineapple, abound in American rainforests, usually perched in the crooks of tree branches. Parrots, macaws and other showy plumed birds are at home in the Pyramid, some of them quite talkative. Sprays of extraordinarily colored phalaenopsis orchids—pale yellow with pink stripes, white with rosy pink lip—cascade from tree branches. When early plant hunters first saw plain white phalaenopsis high up in the rainforest they mistook them for moths, hence the common name "moth orchid."

SAN ANTONIO BOTANICAL GARDEN

The land that would become the San Antonio Botanical Garden was a limestone quarry until 1877, followed by a water works system for the City of San Antonio that was abandoned shortly before the turn of the century. The site was all but forgotten until the 1940s when Mrs. R.R. Witt and Mrs. Joseph Murphy began to talk up their idea of a botanical garden, a dream that would not come true until the official opening May 3, 1980.

The mission of the Botanical Garden, to connect people to the plant world through experience, education and research, is the yardstick by which all changes and additions are measured. The mostly sunken, earth-insulated modules of the Lucile Halsell Conservatory, a 90,000-square foot complex designed by Argentina-born architect Emilio Ambasz and dedicated in 1988, are stunning in the landscape and magical in their ability to let visitors experience many different plant environments from around the world. The Conservatory buildings surround a sunken courtyard with benches and a tropical lagoon with water lilies and other aquatics.

The Texas Native Trail is in complete contrast to the manmade as it demonstrates the distinct and diverse ecology of plant communities endemic to the Hill Country (Edwards Plateau), East Texas Piney Woods and South Texas. Several early Texas homes have been reconstructed on the site, to illustrate the regional aspects and show the impact plants had on daily pioneer life.

Watersaver Lane, a recent third-acre addition at the top of the hill by the Conservatory, features a cluster of miniature cottages landscaped with appropriately small gardens filled with flowering plants that need little or no irrigation during dry spells. Each of the diminutive cottages has its own architectural style and a front yard designed to show visitors how they can create beautiful landscapes that aren't water guzzlers. Drip irrigation, turf bubbler watering techniques, mulches and permeable paving complete the educational component.

Other gardens on the 33 acres vary in style from formal to casual and include the Old-Fashioned Garden, Rose Garden, Sensory Garden for the Blind, Kumamoto En Garden, Sacred Garden, Shade Garden and Ornamental Grass Garden. Four large rectangular display areas are changed out at least four times a year, to celebrate the seasons and give the gardeners a chance to mass colors and contrasting textures. When possible, butterflies are encouraged, by planting their favored flowers (for example, larkspur, pentas, yarrow and angel's trumpet) and larval food (for example, fennel, parsley, dill, sunflower and passionvine).

PLANTS FROM DESERTS TO RAINFORESTS ARE AT HOME IN THE LUCILE HALSELL CONSERVATORY, WHICH IS COMPRISED OF INDIVIDUAL GLASS ENCLOSURES TUCKED INTO THE EARTH. CLIMATE-CONTROLLED ENVIRONMENTS HOUSE EPIPHYTIC PLANTS—ORCHIDS AND BROMELIADS, CACTI AND OTHER SUCCULENTS, EQUATORIAL TROPICALS, CYCADS, TROPICAL FRUITS, FERNS AND AROIDS, INSECTIVORES AND AQUATICS. MOST REMARKABLE IS THE 65-FOOT HIGH FOREST OF PALMS.

ACREAGE: 33 ACRES

SEASONAL BLOOMS: FLOWERS AND FRAGRANCE IN ALL SEASONS, ESPECIALLY IN THE FORMAL AND DISPLAY GARDENS

OTHER ATTRACTIONS: CHANGING DISPLAYS OF ART IN THE GARDEN. RECONSTRUCTED EARLY TEXAS HOUSES ALONG THE TEXAS NATIVE TRAIL

LANDSCAPE ROSES THAT REQUIRE A MINIMUM OF CARE TO LOOK BEAUTIFUL EVERY DAY ARE FEATURED IN THE ROSE GARDEN WITH ITS CENTRAL FOUNTAIN AND STATUARY. CLIMBING ROSES CLAMBER OVER THE PERIMETER FENCING WHILE THE PRIMARY BRICK WALKWAYS LEAD VISITORS TO OTHER FEATURES SUCH AS THE WISTERIA ARBOR.

FOLLOWING ENTRY TO THE BOTANICAL GARDEN THROUGH THE SULLIVAN CARRIAGE HOUSE, VISITORS FIND THEMSELVES IN GERTIE'S GARDEN, A FLAG-STONED TERRACE WITH OPENINGS FOR SHADE TREES AND SEASONAL FLOWERS. ALL PLANT MATERIALS ARE LABELED, THE MAJORITY BEING TEXAS NATIVES OR PLANTS KNOWN TO BE LOCALLY ADAPTED TO THE NORMALLY ARID CLIMATE.

'JOHNNY-JUMP-UPS' OR VIOLAS (NEAR RIGHT) ARE EUROPEAN IN ORIGIN AND, LIKE THEIR BIG COUSINS, THE PANSIES, THRIVE IN THE COOLER SEASONS. THEY FREELY SELF-SOW AND HAVE A WAY OF APPEARING DELIGHTFULLY WHERE YOU'D NEVER THINK TO PLANT THEM.

A BENCH SHELTERED BY THE ROSE GARDEN'S ARBOR (OPPOSITE, LEFT) RECALLS A GARDENER'S LAMENT: "I NEVER HAVE TIME TO SIT, BUT WHAT A NICE IDEA!" LAVISHLY BLOOMING ROSES LIKE THE 'KNOCK OUTS,' WHICH REQUIRE NO DEADHEADING, KEEP THE ROSE GARDEN VISITOR-READY WITH LITTLE UPKEEP.

LOUISIANA IRIS, SUCH AS 'TANAKO' (OPPOSITE, RIGHT), GROW WITH ABANDON BY STREAMS AND PONDS, OFTEN NATURALIZING IN DITCHES WHERE WATER STANDS AT FLOWERING TIME IN THE SPRING. THERE ARE THOUSANDS OF CULTIVARS IN EVERY COLOR IMAGINABLE; 'LOUISIANA' IS SOMEWHAT MISLEADING SINCE THESE IRISES CAN SURVIVE TEMPERATURES BELOW ZERO.

SHIMEK'S GARDENS

Harvey and Nell Shimek have been gardening for years, "A labor of love," she says. First there were lots of roses, tropicals and perennial flowers, all in a country setting a mile outside the city limits of Alvin, an hour's drive south of Houston. Then they planted some daylilies and the rest is history. Soon after word got out about their new interest in daylilies, the Brazosport Daylily Club came to visit and invited the Shimeks to join their merry band.

Almost before they knew it, the couple was hooked. "We decided it would be enjoyable to have a National Display Garden for the American Hemerocallis Society," which means they'd be committed to growing hundreds of different daylilies from breeders all over the country. The guidelines for a National Display Garden for the AHS are simple: Grow the plants as well as possible under local conditions and display each with the name of the breeder and the name of the cultivar in beds that are maintained year-round. And, of course, welcome fellow daylily lovers whenever they call for an appointment to come visit.

Today the Shimeks grow about 850 different cultivars and thousands of their own seedlings, which are the result of dabbling pollen from one bloom onto the pistil of another. A new daylily evolves from each seed that sprouts. "We always look forward to seeing the first blooms on our babies," Nell says. And since not every seedling is unique, better or different from others that have already been named, tough love ensues in deciding which to keep and which to compost.

By now the Shimeks have achieved their original goal, which was to have year-round color in the garden. Both are judges for the American Hemerocallis Society and members of the Lone Star Daylily Society. "Our celebration of daylilies is an ongoing adventure that we practice daily," she says, "a hobby that has gotten completely out of hand." It is something they enjoy together, hoping all the while to pass the love of gardening and plant hybridizing to the grandchildren.

The common name "daylily" applies to plants known botanically as members of the genus *Hemerocallis*, a member of the true lily family. The species and earlier cultivars hold true to the description implied by "daylily," which is to say each flower opens in the morning, closes in the evening and is finished. Some more recently developed cultivars have flowers that may open the evening before and last for 24 hours. Some are also fragrant, some are double and some are re-bloomers.

A HERD OF RESTING LONGHORNS IN A NEIGHBOR'S FIELD PROVIDES THE ULTIMATE IN BORROWED SCENERY. THE DAYLILIES IN THE FOREGROUND SHOW THE ARRAY OF COLORS AND FLOWER FORMS. EXCEPTING WHEN THERE IS A DEEP FREEZE, THE SHIMEKS HAVE SOME DAYLILIES IN BLOOM NEARLY EVERY DAY OF THE YEAR.

ACREAGE: 4.3 ACRES

SEASONAL BLOOMS: SPRING AND SUMMER FOR PEAK BLOOM, BUT SOME COLOR ALMOST EVERY DAY ALL YEAR

SPRING AT SHIMEK'S BRINGS EASTER LILIES AND THE EARLY DAYLILIES, ACCOMPANIED BY A VARIETY OF NATIVE FLOWERS, PERENNIALS, AND ANNUALS THAT FREELY RE-SEED. MOWED GRASS PATHS BETWEEN THE FLOWERBEDS PROVIDE THE SOOTHING GREEN THAT COMPLE-MENTS ALL FLOWER COLORS AND

MAKE STROLLING A DELIGHTFUL PURSUIT. ARBORS AND BENCHES HAVE BEEN THOUGHTFULLY PLACED SO THAT VISITORS CAN PAUSE TO APPRECIATE THE BEST VIEWS.

A RUSTIC SIGN EXPRESSES THE SHIMEKS' PHILOSOPHY, THE DRIVING FORCE BEHIND THEIR PASSION FOR GARDENING AND FOR SHARING WHAT THEY GROW. THE LARGE CLAY POT WITH A SMALLER ONE ON TOP SUGGESTS AN IDEA FOR DOUBLE-DECKER POTS, THE BETTER TO SHOW OFF CASCADING PETUNIAS.

ORANGE COSMOS AND A 'RED MEIDILAND' LANDSCAPE ROSE MAKE A VIVID COMBINATION IN THE SPRINGTIME, BUT SOME BLOOM THROUGH THE SUMMER AND PUT ON A BIGGER SHOW WHEN COOL WEATHER RETURNS AFTER LABOR DAY. 'RED MEIDILAND' HAS ORANGE-RED SEED HIPS THAT LAST INTO WINTER OR UNTIL THE BIRDS DEVOUR THEM.

PURPLE CONEFLOWERS (*Echinacea purpurea*) SELF-SOW WITH ABANDON, FORMING GREAT WAVES OF COLOR IN THE SPRING AND EARLY SUMMER. MANY DIFFERENT CULTIVARS ARE AVAILABLE, INCLUDING SOME THAT HAVE PURE WHITE PETALS, OTHERS CREAMY YELLOW OR APRICOT. IF DEADHEADED, A SECOND, LESSER ROUND OF FLOWERING OCCURS, OTHERWISE BIRDS EAT THE SEEDS AND NO DOUBT ASSIST IN SPREADING THE PLANTS TO OTHER GARDEN SPOTS.

Hidden gingers, known botanically as *curcuma*, grow with abandon at Shimek's Gardens, blooming mostly in the spring and early summer. Because the pink-topped green bracts that display the small yellow flowers grow on stems much shorter than the leaves with their distinctive ruby-red stripe, they are known as hidden gingers.

Curcumas grow best in light shade, moist, well-drained soil and tropical temperatures.

SOUTH TEXAS BOTANICAL GARDEN AND NATURE CENTER

Corpus Christi, from the Latin for Body of Christ, also known as the Sparkling City by the Sea, has a population of about 300,000, making it Texas's eighth-largest urban center. Since it first opened in 1996, the South Texas Botanical Gardens and Nature Center has become one of the area's most popular visitor destinations. At the outset there was the Children's Garden, Bird and Butterfly Trail, Palapa Grande on Gator Lake and Visitors' Center. This modest beginning soon took a giant step forward with the addition of a four-wing Exhibit House and the Don Larkin Memorial Orchid Greenhouse, home to some 3,500 orchids tended by members of the South Texas Orchid Society. The Orchid House climate, controlled by fans, heaters and a wet wall, also has rainwater collection, reverse osmosis and mist systems.

The semi-arid to semitropical Corpus Christi climate is famously windy, yet proximity to the Gulf keeps temperatures to the high 90s in the summer and winter lows stay mostly above freezing. Compared to many places in Texas—and the world for that matter—it is a gardener's paradise, a reality that fosters the continued growth of the South Texas Botanical Gardens. Recent additions include a Sensory Garden, more than 250 plumerias planted around the Exhibit House by the Plumeria Society of South Texas, a Rose Garden, Hibiscus Garden, Wetlands Awareness Boardwalk, Arid Garden and Tree Demonstration Garden. Also in the works are production greenhouses, a Hummingbird Garden, Tropical Garden and Wetlands Interpretive Center.

Within the 180 acres there are also seemingly endless bike and nature trails, outlooks for birders and boardwalks that allow exploration of the wetlands without disturbing the ecosystem.

As an example of the Gardens' educational outreach, members of the Corpus Christi Rose Society conduct a workshop in late September to demonstrate proper pruning to get the most blooms. Pruning at this time leads to a major flowering all through fall and sometimes right into winter.

Two stone benches in the Rose Garden are of particular note. The work of local artist Danny O'Dowdy, they consist of limestone rocks brought in from the Texas Hill Country and carved into the shapes of sofas. Grouted mosaic tiles represent upholstery, in colorful designs inspired by Mexican sarapes. While they look soft, couch potatoes take note: Do not plop down on these sofas, rather sit slowly and deliberately.

THE 30-BY 40-FOOT ROSE GARDEN PAVILION WAS COMPLETED IN 2002, AND IS HOME TO MORE THAN 300 ROSES CARED FOR BY VOLUNTEERS FROM THE CORPUS CHRISTI ROSE SOCIETY. THE BENCH, BY LOCAL ARTIST DANNY O'DOWDY, IS CREATED FROM LIMESTONE BLOCKS CARVED INTO THE SHAPE OF A SOFA, WITH CERAMIC TILE "UPHOLSTERY" EVOCATIVE OF A MEXICAN SARAPE.

ACREAGE: 180 ACRES

SEASONAL BLOOMS: ROSES IN SPRING AND FALL; HIBISCUS AND PLUMERIAS IN SUMMER; ORCHIDS ALL YEAR

OTHER ATTRACTIONS MESQUITE FOREST: BIRD AND BUTTERFLY TRAIL; BIRDING TOWER; WETLANDS AWARENESS BOARDWALK

A massive Rose Garden Fountain stands in front of the tile-roofed Rose Garden Pavilion. The Rose Garden, with its 12 raised planting beds, was designed by landscape architect Robert Gignac. Red-and-white striped roses have been popular since the 17th century. 'Scentimental,' a cluster-flowered floribunda introduced in 1997, has double flowers to nearly 5 inches across that have old rose fragrance laced with spice.

Native and locally adapted salvias such as 'Indigo Spires' grow with abandon in the South Texas Botanical Gardens, attracting bees, birds and butterflies. Flagstone paths meander through the plantings, which offer something of beauty every day in all seasons.

STEPHEN F. AUSTIN MAST ARBORETUM AND PINEYWOODS NATIVE PLANT CENTER

Located on the north side of the Stephen F. Austin State University campus, the Stephen F. Austin Mast Arboretum was founded in 1985, thus making it the state's first arboretum at a university. A more lasting and important distinction is that its leader, Dr. David Creech, is a genius plantsman with a sense of humor to match, revealed in his nutshell description of the Arboretum: "…where good design never got in our way…what the garden is (cool) and is not (refined). Best of the best and worst of the worst of plants and showcase gardens. Diversity rules." He signs his communications, "Keep planting."

And keep planting is exactly what Dr. Creech, the staff and the volunteers have been doing from the outset. Most notable is the Ruby Mize Azalea Garden, an 8-acre public garden built between 1997 and 2001 as home to 6,500 azaleas, 200 camellias (including 21 bred by a 1930s SFASU Agriculture graduate Hody Wilson), 200 different Japanese maples, 180 varieties of hydrangea and a plant lover's phantasmagorical array of 400 odd and rare trees and shrubs. Or, as Dr. Creech says, "More strange plants in one spot than is normally allowed by the authorities."

Connected by over a mile of trails, the 46 beds that are home to the collections have been planted with the key objective to have color all year. This has been achieved in part by selecting repeat-blooming azaleas, cultivars that bloom in the summer and fall, not just in the spring when a green thumb is hardly necessary to achieve color. The plants have also been selected for adaptability to acidic soil (pH 5.8-6.5), USDA Hardiness Zone 8b and the American Horticulture Society's Heat Zone 9, including average annual rainfall of 46 inches, seasonal flooding and a protracted 240-day summer marked by scorching heat and withering humidity.

The Arboretum's mission is a model that in spirit could wisely be followed by any group aspiring to create a public garden that is both educational and a show place: 1) Promote the conservation, selection and use of the native plants of Texas; 2) Acquire, evaluate and promote new and adapted landscape plants and promote plant diversity in the landscape; 3) Serve as a living laboratory for SFA students and faculty, the nursery and landscape industry; 4) Provide an aesthetic and educational environment for students, visitors and local citizens.

Finally, a couple of bon mots from the Arboretum's printed matter: "It takes one hundred years to build a garden; two hundred years if you don't intend to rush it… Open free dawn to dusk—take only pictures, leave only footprints."

A MONARCH BUTTERFLY FINDS A BEAUTIFUL PLACE TO DINE ON A FLAME AZALEA IN EARLY SPRING. AMERICAN NATIVE DECIDUOUS AZALEAS OF THIS TYPE PROVIDE NECTAR FOR BUTTERFLIES AND THEY ARE ALSO OFTEN FRAGRANT. (OVERLEAF) MARCH AND APRIL BRING PEAK BLOOM IN THE RUBY MIZE AZALEA GARDEN WHERE MORE THAN 6,000 DIFFERENT AZALEAS, BOTH HYBRID EVERGREEN AND NATIVE DECIDUOUS, GROW IN THE MIDST OF A 50-YEAR-OLD LOBLOLLY PINE FOREST.

ACREAGE: 10 ACRES

SEASONAL BLOOMS: CAMELLIAS IN WINTER; AZALEAS IN SPRING, SUMMER AND FALL; HYDRANGEAS IN SUMMER

OTHER ATTRACTIONS: SEMINARS AND LECTURE SERIES WITH OUTSTANDING SPEAKERS

(PREVIOUS PAGE) BESIDES AZALEAS, THE SANDY LOAM SOIL OF THE LaNANA CREEK FLOODPLAIN FAVORS A COLLECTION OF 200 CAMELLIAS, 200 JAPANESE MAPLES, 180 HYDRANGEAS AND MORE THAN 400 ORNAMENTAL WOODY PLANTS.

For a garden comprised of several acres, paving is essential, both for the gardeners' vehicles and for public access. Signage is also important so visitors can know what they admire, take notes and then be prepared to make intelligent requests at the nursery. The Arboretum's design is a model for demonstrating how different plant communities work together—the tallest or canopy trees such as loblolly pines, the shorter or understory trees such as Japanese maples that need some shade, and the groundcovers and shrubs—azaleas, camellias, hydrangeas—that need full to dappled shade in summer.

TEXAS A&M HORTICULTURAL GARDEN

The Texas A&M Horticultural Garden is designed to be educational for students as well as the general public, which is to say, the scale and size of the many demonstration gardens easily translate to a home yard. Beginning at Visitor Parking there is a display of ornamental grasses, which are planted for their all-season beauty and simplistic care; plant them at almost any time and do nothing but cut the old growth to the ground in the spring.

Next in an orderly visit is the Hill Country Garden, with old-fashioned natives and locally adapted plants that make you glad but require little work; the Trellis Garden demonstrates a variety of hardy and sometimes fragrant vines—clematis, honeysuckle, trumpet vine, passion vine and others; Found Roses, the sorts of heirlooms and antiques made famous by the Texas Rose Rustlers; the Xeriscape and West Texas Garden, with plantings designed to need no irrigation except when newly planted; and, in refreshing contrast, the Water Garden and the Shade Garden. At this point in your tour you can wander off to the Natural Habitat Area, a wonderland for birders—or go the opposite direction and visit the Texas Perennial Border, which has many plants that attract butterflies, bees and hummingbirds.

There are four gardens of special interest: The Enabling Garden has different plant beds and seating areas to illustrate how anyone with a sincere desire to garden can do so, regardless of ability or disability. There are raised beds for wheelchair gardeners, vertical gardens for persons who have had a stroke or are paralyzed from other causes, beds with seating on the edges to accommodate arthritic joints—all with dimensions that make the garden wheelchair friendly.

The Warren and Margaret Barham Heritage Garden showcases vegetables, herbs, fruits, ornamentals and antique roses. The garden also includes rain lilies, purple sage and hardy hibiscus with Texas-size flowers. It is centered by a circa 1850 Texas cottage that serves as the tool and supply shed. The garden honors Dr. Barham, first department head of Horticulture at Texas A&M.

The Kitchen Garden is a 20-by 20-foot fenced (against rabbits) pattern garden of edible plants that are replanted seasonally, in order to feature cool-season and warm-season crops. Herbs, cactus (*nopales*) and edible flowers grow in a central bed. The Children's Discovery Trail shows the garden's ecosystem and how it can affect our lives. Three large displays illustrate xeric or dry ecosystems, mesic or moist ecosystems, and hydric or wet ecosystems. One section of the trail is an active organic garden, which helps children understand how healthy gardens can grow without the use of synthetic fertilizers and pesticides.

ONLY AN AGGIE—AND MAYBE GEORGIA O'KEEFFE—WOULD ORNAMENT A GARDEN WITH A BOVINE SKULL AND A BARBED-WIRE WREATH, DISPLAYED WITHIN THE LACY FLOWERING BRANCHES OF THE YELLOW BIRD-OF-PARADISE TREE (*Caesalpinia gilliesii*).

ACREAGE: 15 ACRES

SEASONAL BLOOMS: PRIMARILY SPRING THROUGH FALL, BUT THERE IS ALWAYS SOMETHING OF INTEREST EVEN IN WINTER

OTHER ATTRACTIONS: CLASSES AND WORKSHOPS ABOUT ALL PHASES OF GARDENING, LANDSCAPING AND FLORISTRY

A PRIMARY PURPOSE OF THE GARDEN IS TO DEMONSTRATE GARDENING PRACTICES THAT ADDRESS "GREEN" ISSUES IN A PRACTICAL WAY: WATER, WATER QUALITY, WATER CONSERVATION, INTEGRATED PEST MANAGEMENT, AND SELF-RELIANT LANDSCAPES THAT ARE REWARDING, NOT BACK BREAKING. HARDY PERENNIAL DIANTHUS, LANDSCAPE ROSES AND SELF-SEEDING LARKSPUR BLOOM RELIABLY WITHOUT FUSS.

BOG PLANTS GROW AROUND THE
WATER-LILY POND, PART OF THE
PROGRAM TO DEMONSTRATE
WATER MANAGEMENT AND THE
IMPORTANCE OF WETLANDS. THE
WATER-SPOUTING CRANES ARE A
CONSTANT REMINDER THAT IN
ORDER TO HAVE SONG BIRDS IN A
GARDEN, IT IS NECESSARY TO
PROVIDE CONSTANT FRESH WATER,
AS WELL AS PLANTINGS FOR COVER
THAT PROVIDE SEEDS AND BERRIES
AS A FOOD SOURCE.

ONCE ESTABLISHED, CANNAS RETURN YEAR AFTER YEAR, REQUIRING DIVISION AND REPLANTING ONLY AFTER SEVERAL GROWING SEASONS. CANNAS OFTEN NATURALIZE IN DITCHES OR OTHER PLACES THAT ARE OCCASIONALLY INUNDATED WITH WATER DURING THE GROWING SEASON.

BOTTLEBRUSH OR *callistemon* (UPPER RIGHT) IS AN EVERGREEN SHRUB OR SMALL TREE FROM AUSTRALIA THAT ADAPTS WELL TO WARM, DRY CLIMATES IN THE UNITED STATES. THE BOTTLEBRUSH FLOWERS APPEAR IN SPRING AND SUMMER, FOLLOWING A COOL BUT ESSENTIALLY FROST-FREE WINTER.

IN COLDER CLIMATES, BOTTLE-BRUSH MAKES AN IDEAL CONTAINER PLANT THAT CAN BE WINTERED IN ANY SUNNY WINDOW WITH MODERATELY COOL TEMPERATURES, 50-60 DEGREES BEING IDEAL.

A BLUE CENTURY PLANT OR AGAVE, (OPPOSITE PAGE) IS SURROUNDED BY TEXAS BLUEBONNETS. THE SUCCULENT NATURE OF AGAVES ALLOWS THEM TO SURVIVE DROUGHT. THEY SEND UP A TOWERING FLOWER STALK AFTER 25 TO 30 YEARS, PRODUCE SEEDS AND OFFSETS, THEN DIE.

TEXAS DISCOVERY GARDENS

The Texas Discovery Gardens is the second oldest botanical institution in Texas, dating to 1936, and, in 2003, the first certified 100-percent organic public garden in the state. It probably also holds the record for having the most name changes, despite the fact its location at historic Fair Park and primary mission has never changed. The aim is to be a year-round urban oasis where natural wonders delight and pique the curiosity of visitors of all ages.

There are ten themed areas focusing on butterfly habitats, a native wildlife pond, a scent garden, shade garden and a living history garden of heirloom plants. A particular strength of today's Texas Discovery Gardens is its outreach to families, to show parents and children how they can use native and adapted plants to create backyard habitats that will attract butterflies, song birds and other wildlife.

Patterned after an English herb garden, the Scent Garden was first built in 1958 as a project of the Marianne Scruggs Garden Club. At the outset it was designed as an outreach to the visually handicapped. At the beginning of the 21st century, the City of Dallas renovated the garden using bond funds and visitors of all stripes are encouraged to experience it with all the senses.

The new name—Texas Discovery Gardens—was adopted in 2000 and the mission statement re-worded to suit the new century: "To have a positive impact on the future of Texas by teaching effective ways to restore, conserve and preserve nature in the urban environment through the use of native and adapted plants which illustrate the interrelationship of butterflies, bugs and botany."

As of 2008 the Texas Discovery Gardens Conservatory and Main Building is being renovated under the guidance of Oglesby Greene, Architects. The culmination will be a new permanent all-year attraction: The Rosine Smith Sammons Butterfly House and Insectarium. Slated to open in the late summer of 2009, it will house thousands of exotic butterflies and insects in a natural environment designed to be both educational and entertaining.

By any name, each generation who has donated gifts of self and money to the institution now known as the Texas Discovery Gardens has sought the help of the most talented garden and landscape designers, architects and artists that could be found. Joe Lambert, for example, who created the Callier Garden, Leftwich Reflecting Pool and Circular Lawn in the 1960s and 1970s, was one of the most respected landscape architects of the time.

THE HALL OF HORTICULTURE OPENED IN 1938 AND WAS DESIGNATED FOR USE BY THE DALLAS GARDEN CENTER, WHICH WAS CHARTERED IN 1941. THE MAIN HALL, ADDED IN 1958, CREATED A MUCH NEEDED SPACE FOR GARDEN CLUB FLOWER SHOWS. "CIVIC" WAS ADDED TO THE NAME IN 1982, FOLLOWED BY A COMPLETE CHANGE IN 1994 TO DALLAS HORTICULTURE CENTER AND FINALLY TODAY'S GENERATION HAS SETTLED ON TEXAS DISCOVERY GARDENS.

ACREAGE: 7.5 ACRES

SEASONAL BLOOMS: AZALEAS AND BULBS IN SPRING, FOLLOWED BY ROSES; TROPICAL BLOOMS AND COLORFUL FOLIAGE IN SUMMER; ROSES AND CHRYSANTHEMUMS IN THE FALL; HOLLIES IN WINTER

OTHER ATTRACTIONS: MUSIC, THEATER, MUSEUMS, PICNICKING, ATHLETIC PURSUITS, ALL IN FAIR PARK

DALLAS WAS AMONG THE FIRST CITIES TO EMBRACE MODERNIST SCULPTURE (ABOVE), THE PRESENCE OF WHICH HAS BEEN INTEGRAL TO THE PERSONALITY OF THE TEXAS DISCOVERY GARDENS FROM THE OUTSET.

A LANDSCAPE ARCHITECT OF RENOWN, JOE LAMBERT, DESIGNED THE CALLIER GARDEN, LEFTWICH REFLECTING POOL AND CIRCULAR LAWN IN THE 1960s AND 1970s. LAMBERT WAS GIFTED IN EXPRESSING THE CLASSIC LANDSCAPE ARCHITECTURE OF WESTERN EUROPE USING TREES AND OTHER PLANTS THAT WOULD THRIVE IN NORTH TEXAS.

TYLER MUNICIPAL ROSE GARDEN

Sandy soils, relatively generous annual rainfall and a moderate climate have made the area around Tyler in East Texas a center for growing vegetables, fruits and flowers, in particular roses, since before the Civil War. Rose lovers the world over know about Tyler roses and today the 14 acres that comprise the Tyler Municipal Rose Garden make it the country's largest. Altogether there are more than 38,000 rosebushes representing at least 500 different varieties—from miniatures with perfectly formed hybrid-tea shaped blossoms the size of a dime to stately tree-form standard roses, each gained by grafting onto the rootstock the trunk and grafted on top of it the cultivar chosen to be the flowering head.

Of primary interest is the part of the garden that serves as one of 24 official sites for testing new roses vying for the honor of being named an All-America Rose Selection. Visitors have the opportunity to consider test roses identified by code numbers only, as well as winners with names and the coveted distinction of wearing the AARS insignia. Second, there is a garden of David Austin English Roses, which was added in 2000, and includes 300 of these recently developed varieties that look like old-fashioned roses having a multitude of petals in luscious colors, voluptuous fragrance and ever-blooming habit. Third is the Heritage and Sensory Garden comprised of antique roses and perennial flowers, which represents a cooperative effort between the Gertrude Windsor Garden Club, the Smith County Master Gardeners, Doctor Brent Pemberton and the Tyler Parks Department. This garden demonstrates the latest thinking about roses—that they needn't be isolated in hedged, formal beds, but may be combined with hardy perennial flowers and ornamental grasses.

The rose gardens are open from dawn to dusk, seven days a week, and admission is free. The gardens and the Rose Garden Center can also be rented for special events. There is an admission fee to visit the Tyler Rose Museum, a 7,500 square-foot facility that reflects both the commercial horticulture that has made Tyler synonymous with roses and the history of the town itself.

In order to produce a big show of roses for the Texas Rose Festival held here in mid-October each year, considerable pruning is done around Labor Day, which means, if you have a choice, September is probably not the best month to visit. The Festival attracts thousands intent on taking time to smell the roses, as well as to meet the Rose Queen and partake of the Queen's Tea.

MANICURED GRASS CARPETS MAKE A PLUSH SETTING FOR BEDS OF ROSES, ARRANGED IN ROWS BY VARIETY. 'MR. LINCOLN,' A HYBRID TEA INTRODUCED IN 1964 AND NAMED AN ALL-AMERICA ROSE SELECTION IN 1965, IS TALL, DARK RED AND INTENSELY FRAGRANT—ATTRIBUTES THAT HAVE MADE IT A FAVORITE CHOICE IN CONVERSATIONS DEVOTED TO THE SUBJECT OF, "IF I COULD HAVE ONLY ONE ROSE."

ACREAGE: 14 ACRES

SEASONAL BLOOMS: SOME ROSES THROUGHOUT THE GROWING SEASON; PEAK BLOOMS MID-SPRING TO EARLY SUMMER; LATE SEPTEMBER THROUGH OCTOBER

OTHER ATTRACTIONS: ROSE MUSEUM; ROSE FESTIVAL IN MID-OCTOBER

The sights and mingled fragrances from 14 acres and 38,000 roses defy description, although words such as awesome, fantastic, fabulous and knee-bending come to mind. New varieties being tested, All-American Selections and the David Austin English roses grow in beds unto themselves. The antique or heritage roses are gardened with hardy perennial flowers, to show visitors how they might combine these plants at home and in so doing practice the latest trend in gardening.

Opposite, clockwise from upper left: Grandiflora 'Queen Elizabeth,' AARS 1955, remains one of the most popular large-flowered hybrids; hybrid tea 'Sheer Bliss,' AARS 1987, is tea-scented; hybrid tea 'Mr. Lincoln,' AARS 1965, is both strong-growing and heavily scented; hybrid tea 'Tropicana,' AARS 1963, has a fruity sweet smell and the glowing orange color has made it a perennial favorite.

VICTORIA MEMORIAL ROSE GARDEN

The historic city of Victoria, situated about equidistant—around a hundred miles—from Houston, Austin, San Antonio and Corpus Christi, is 25 miles from Port Lavaca and the Gulf of Mexico. First established in 1685, Victoria became the third city chartered in Texas in 1824, under the leadership of Martin DeLeon, who called it "Nuestra De Guadalupe De Victoria." The original settlement was planned around a market square in the manner of most European and Mexican cities. Today it is the downtown's center and is known as DeLeon Plaza. The surrounding original township of 256 blocks contains over 2,000 historic references, among them over a hundred structures listed in the National Register of Historic Places.

Modern Victoria has 12 parks, the largest being Riverside Park, which is made up of 562 acres along the Guadalupe River. Besides the Rose Garden, Riverside Park has a 27-hole public golf course, a trail for exercisers, a public dock for boaters, the Texas Zoo (6 acres and more than 150 Texas native animals), a duck pond next to a beautiful gazebo and an abundance of playgrounds and places outfitted for picnicking. Riverside Stadium hosts baseball games and tournaments and there is also the Horseman's Club.

The Rose Garden, located on McCright Drive in Riverside Park, is home to more than a thousand rosebushes representing at least a hundred different varieties. Framed by pristine white fencing, the roses are accompanied by an imposing water fountain and pool, a gazebo and arbor, with paved walkways that make the garden accessible for strollers and wheelchairs.

The Victoria Rose Garden is one of only seven public rose gardens in Texas accredited by the American Rose Society, a designation that recognizes the high quality of horticulture, the clear interpretive signage and the choice of roses that are suited to the climate. The most abundant flowering occurs in the spring months and again in the fall, the times when temperatures by day are warm and at night are cool. The most heat-tolerant roses continue blooming in the summer and some manage to bloom through the brief, normally mild winter season.

SEEN WITH THE GARDEN'S GAZEBO IN THE DISTANCE, A FULLY OPEN FLOWER OF 2005 ALL-AMERICA ROSE SELECTIONS WINNER 'ABOUT FACE' REVEALS A SUBTLE COMBINATION OF GOLDEN-ORANGE AND PALE BRONZY RED. A LARGE-FLOWERED HYBRID OR GRANDIFLORA ROSE, IT GROWS TALL AND STURDILY UPRIGHT WITH MEDIUM-LARGE, FULLY DOUBLE FLOWERS THAT SMELL LIKE FRESH-CUT APPLE.

ACREAGE: 5 ACRES

SEASONAL BLOOMS: PEAK BLOOM TIMES IN SPRING AND FALL, BUT SOME ROSES ALSO IN SUMMER AND WINTER

OTHER ATTRACTIONS: RIVERSIDE PARK'S 562 ACRES OFFER OPPORTUNITIES FOR FISHING, GOLF, HIKING, BIKING, VISITING THE TEXAS ZOO, PICNICKING AND PLAYGROUNDS

First introduced in 1972, 'Gypsy,' a modern, cluster-flowered rose, has unusually large, spice-scented flowers over a long season. It makes a long-lasting cut flower, often creating a bouquet on one stem.

Tea-scented 'Betty Prior,' a shrub rose introduced in 1935, is much loved for its resemblance to a wild rose. The more recent 'Pink Meidiland' is similar but more vivid. 'Coral Meidiland' and 'Coral Knock Out' express the same conformation, but in a coral-pink color.

A CLASSIC TRIPLE FOUNTAIN CENTERS
A REFLECTING POOL SURROUNDED
BY BEDS OF ROSES THAT LINE THE
PAVED STROLLING PATHS. A MORN-
ING VISIT AFTER THE SUN RAYS
HAVE WARMED THE ESSENTIAL OILS
IS THE BEST TIME TO SMELL THE
ROSES. BESIDES "TRUE" ROSE SCENT,
THEY MAY ALSO SMELL FRUITY,
LEMONY, SPICY OR OF SWEET
VIOLET (*Viola odorata*).

WHITE FENCING AND A LATTICE ARBOR FOR CLIMBING ROSES MAKE A PICTURESQUE SETTING FOR A CLASSIC ROSE GARDEN. MODERN ROSES BRED FOR THE COMMERCIAL CUT-FLOWER TRADE ARE OFTEN NOT FRAGRANT, SINCE PRODUCING FRAGRANCE TAKES ENERGY THE BREEDERS PRAGMATICALLY DIRECT TOWARD LONG SHELF LIFE. THE SAME IS NOT TRUE OF GARDEN ROSES, WHICH ARE MORE LIKELY TO ACHIEVE SUCCESS IN THE MARKETPLACE IF THEY ARE BOTH DISEASE-RESISTANT AND FRAGRANT.

THE WATER GARDENS AT FOUNTAIN PLACE

As great public gardens go, the Water Gardens at Fountain Place in Dallas and Bryant Park in New York City have more in common than might be suspected. Planning for Water Fountain Gardens began in 1982, construction in 1984 and completion took place in 1986. Bryant Park's history, dating from 1686, is not nearly so tidy, yet the planning that led to its reincarnation and reopening in 1992 was also begun in the 1980s. While Bryant Park is almost an acre larger than Water Fountain Gardens, both places serve the same purpose: to provide an oasis where thousands of workers whose offices are in neighboring skyscrapers can reconnect with nature, take a break, eat some lunch, catch a few rays of sun and maybe even seal a business deal.

Each space is a design masterpiece of its type. Bryant Park's site plan by Hanna-Olin, which features a large open lawn with herbaceous perennial borders by Lynden Miller in the grand European manner, is entirely in keeping with the Beaux-Arts architecture of the New York Public Library behind which it stands. Dan Kiley's grid-based design for Water Gardens at the foot of Pei Cobb Freed & Partners' sparkling, glass-clad skyscraper, is the epitome of modern landscape architecture.

Simplicity is the order of the day in Kiley's work, evidenced in the Water Gardens as concrete terraces over which water cascades around a circular planter for each bald cypress tree. Historically, garden and landscape designers have not arranged trees in a grid except in orchards, which infuses Kiley's grid of bald cypress trees with a certain symbolism of fruitfulness.

Water Fountain Gardens also has an area of marble paving arranged in the manner of a linear vegetable garden, with holes cut in the marble through which water spouts up periodically. Children love to play in this area, hoping to get sprayed, and an occasional unsuspecting business-suited adult gets an unwelcome shower. While the setting is modern landscape architecture, the idea of fantastic water jets is centuries old. Even in the most serious garden architecture of classical Greece and Rome, the unwary could be soaked at the turn of a tap. At Water Fountain Park the jets are synchronized, so it doesn't take long for an observant visitor to figure out when to expect the next water show.

AS CONTEMPORARY AS TOMORROW, YET AS OLD IN SPIRIT AS ITALIAN AND FRENCH BAROQUE, WATER IN THE FOUNTAIN GARDENS SPILLS OVER TERRACED CONCRETE AROUND CONTAINERIZED BALD CYPRESS TREES. CLOSE-BY, WATER SPOUTS UP PERIODICALLY THROUGH HOLES IN MARBLE PAVING, GIVING UNSUSPECTING VISITORS A SHOWER AND DELIGHTING CHILDREN, THUS RECALLING THE WATER JOKES AND JETS EMPLOYED BY ANCIENT GREEK AND ROMAN GARDEN ARCHITECTS.

ACREAGE: 2.1 ACRES

SEASONAL BLOOMS: BALD CYPRESS TREES, GREEN EXCEPT IN WINTER

OTHER ATTRACTIONS: SPECTACULAR ARCHITECTURE ON A FULL CITY BLOCK

A LITTLE MORE THAN 2 ACRES OF FOUNTAIN PLACE'S 5.5 ACRES, AT THE NORTHERN EDGE OF THE CITY'S CENTRAL BUSINESS DISTRICT, ARE DEVOTED TO THE WATER GARDENS, DESIGNED BY LANDSCAPE ARCHITECT DAN KILEY. THE ARRANGEMENT OF BALD CYPRESS TREES IN AN ORCHARD-LIKE GRID IS CONSISTENT WITH KILEY'S VISION OF PUBLIC GARDENS EXPERIENCED AS SERENE SPACES IN STARK CONTRAST TO THE CHAOTIC WORLD AT LARGE.

THE 60-STORY OFFICE TOWER AT
FOUNTAIN PLACE, BY ARCHITECTS
PEI COBB FREED & PARTNERS,
LEAD DESIGNER HENRY N. COBB,
CONTAINS 1.3 MILLION SQUARE
FEET OF OFFICE SPACE. COMPLETED
IN 1986, THE GOAL WAS A UNIQUE
SKYLINE PRESENCE AND AN
INVITING PUBLIC SPACE AT STREET
LEVEL. HALF OF THE BUILDING
VOLUME IS CARVED AWAY FROM
THE BASE TO A HEIGHT OF 60 FEET
TO ACCOMMODATE THE WATER
GARDEN AND ORDERLY FOREST OF
BALD CYPRESS TREES.

ZILKER BOTANICAL GARDEN

The Garden Center in what would become the Zilker Botanical Garden had its beginnings in 1946 when the Violet Crown Garden Club set aside $50 they'd earned from the sale of firewood, a seemingly modest move that sparked more fund-raising by seven garden clubs that became the Austin Area Garden Council in 1955. The original building was completed in 1964 and by 1996 the Garden Council had grown to 39 clubs representing 2,000 members, at which point they and the City undertook a massive renovation of the facility.

By collaborating with the City of Austin, the garden club members have made the Zilker Botanical Gardens a thriving entity that hosts some 300,000 visitors each year. The Garden Center is the site of as many as 50 monthly meetings where individuals of all ages can learn about plants and sustainable gardening practices.

Of special note is the Isamu Taniguchi Japanese Garden, which opened to the public in 1969 following 18 months of labor donated by the 70-year-old Taniguchi, who transformed 3 acres of rugged caliche hillside into a peaceful garden. A Japanese teahouse and stone gates have been added, along with stone retaining walls to contain a collection of different bamboos.

The Mabel Davis Rose Garden, dedicated in 1973, features all kinds of roses suited to Austin gardens and is now an official All-America Rose Selections display garden. Subsequent structural embellishments include the Bickler Cupola that originally topped one of the first Austin public schools, the Carl Von Bleucher Memorial Columns that are home to climbing roses, the Rose Memorial Arch and the Anschi Wilson Memorial Rose Arbor with a stone plaza and redwood seating.

In keeping with its mission to inspire and inform individuals of all ages who visit, the Zilker includes the Doug Blachly Butterfly Trail and Garden, a Pioneer Village with an Organic Garden, a Herb Garden that has lately been enlarged to accommodate the Vee Fowler Native Texas Herb Garden, a Cactus and Succulent Garden featuring mostly West Texas natives and the Freda Bodine Caladium Garden.

So as to capture and reflect the interest of all visiting gardeners, there is the Posey Perennial Garden, the Daylily Beds and the Iris Beds, which show off collections of tall bearded iris, spuria iris and Louisiana iris. The Endemic Bed lets visitors experience firsthand some of the uncommon native plants they might only otherwise encounter fleetingly while driving. A charming personality trait of the Zilker is its penchant for repurposing architectural salvage and artifacts—giving it the reputation as "the attic of Austin."

A POND AND STREAM IS HOME TO FROLICKING KOI AND OTHER FISH. WATER-LOVING PERENNIALS FOUND IN SHALLOW WATER OR AT THE EDGES OF PONDS—PICKEREL-WEED OR PONTEDERIA, FOR EXAMPLE—THRIVE HERE. THE ROCK-CLAD ISLAND IS HOME TO AN OLD SPECIMEN OF TEXAS WISTERIA (*Wisteria frutescens*), WHICH IS LESS AGGRESSIVE THAN THE ASIAN SPECIES AND PRODUCES ITS FRAGRANT FLOWERS AFTER LEAFING OUT IN THE EARLY SPRING.

ACREAGE: 31 ACRES

SEASONAL BLOOMS: ANNUALS IN WINTER, A WEALTH OF FLOWERS IN SPRING, COLORFUL TROPICALS IN SUMMER, ROSES AND CHRYSANTHEMUMS IN THE FALL

OTHER ATTRACTIONS: ZILKER PARK'S 351 ACRES HOST LIVE MUSIC AND THEATRE, A SWIMMING POOL AND SPORTS FIELDS, AS WELL AS THE AUSTIN NATURE AND SCIENCE CENTER

Each mature leaf of some tropical water-lilies (left) produces an entirely new plant, a duplicate of the parent. All water-lilies are vigorous growers that need sun, fertile soil and regular applications of fertilizer.

The Zilker's varied topography (left) on the south bank of the Colorado River makes it ideal for depicting different habitats and displaying an array of both native and exotic plants.

In the Isamu Taniguchi Japanese Garden, the Togetsu-kyo bridge (opposite) or "Bridge To Walk Over the Moon," is in theory positioned so that when the moon is high, it reflects in the water and follows the person crossing the bridge.

186

TROPICAL WATER-LILIES BLOOM ALL THROUGH THE WARMER MONTHS IN THE WILLIE BIRGE MEMORIAL POND, WHICH WAS DONATED BY THE FAMILY OF MS. BIRGE, AND DEDICATED MAY 1, 1966, TO HONOR THE ONE-TIME DIRECTOR OF BIOLOGY AT DENTON COLLEGE IN NORTH TEXAS. WATER IN THE POND, DESPITE BEING UNFILTERED AND NON-CIRCULATING, IS REMARKABLY WELL MAINTAINED BY AUSTIN POND SOCIETY VOLUNTEERS. THERE ARE BOTH DAY- AND NIGHT-BLOOMING TROPICAL WATER-LILIES, AND SOME ARE FRAGRANT.

THE REDBUD (ABOVE) IS AN AMERICAN NATIVE TREE THAT BLOOMS IN EARLY SPRING ON BOTH NEW AND OLD WOOD, INCLUDING ALONG THE TRUNK. PLANTINGS ALONG A NATIVE STONE WALKWAY (RIGHT) THAT IS BOTH WHEEL-CHAIR- AND STROLLER-FRIENDLY FEATURE TEXAS NATIVE TREES AND FLOWERS.

INDEX

WEBSITES

Alvin: Shimek's Gardens, www.hal-pc.org/~neshimek/Shimek's%20Open%20Garden.htm

Amarillo: Amarillo Botanical Gardens, www.amarillobotanicalgardens.org

Athens: The East Texas Arboretum and Botanical Society, www.eastexasarboretum.org

Austin: The Lady Bird Johnson Wildflower Center, www.wildflower.org

Austin: Zilker Botanical Garden, www.zilkergarden.org

Austin: Charles Umlauf Sculpture Gardens, www.umlaufsculpture.org

Beaumont: Beaumont Botanical Gardens, www.beaumontbotanicalgardens.com

Brenham: Antique Rose Emporium, www.antiqueroseemporium.com

College Station: Texas A & M Horticultural Garden,
  http://aggiehorticulture.tamu.edu/greenhouse/hortgardens/index.html

Corpus Christi: South Texas Botanical Garden and Nature Center, www.stxbot.org

Dallas: The Dallas Arboretum, www.dallasarboretum.org

Dallas: Texas Discovery Gardens, www.texasdiscoverygardens.org

Dallas: The Water Gardens at Fountain Place, www.fountainplace.com

El Paso: The El Paso Desert Botanical Garden at Keystone Heritage Park, www.elpasobotanicalgardens.org

El Paso: The El Paso Municipal Rose Garden, www.elpasotexas.gov

Fort Worth: The Forth Worth Botanic Gardens, www.fwbg.org

Galveston: Moody Gardens, www.moodygardens.com

Hale Center: Bell Park Cacti Gardens, www.lone-star.net/mall/txtrails/hale.htm

Harlingen: Hugh Ramsey Nature Park,
  www.tpwd.state.tx.us/huntwild/wild/wildlife_trails/coastal/lower/losloros/

Houston: Hermann Park, www.hermannpark.org

Houston: The Cullen Sculpture Garden at the MFA, www.mfah.org/sculpturegarden

Houston: Houston Arboretum and Nature Center, www.houstonarboretum.org

Houston: Bayou Bend Gardens, www.mfah.org/bayoubend

Humble: Mercer Arboretum, www.hcp4.net/Mercer

Katy: Forbidden Gardens, www.forbidden-gardens.com

Lubbock: Lubbock Memorial Arboretum, www.lubbockarboretum.org

Mineral Wells: Clark Gardens Botanical Park, www.clarkgardens.com

Nacogdoches: Stephen F. Austin Mast Arboretum, www.arboretum.sfasu.edu

San Antonio: Brackenridge Park Japanese Tea Garden, www.wildtexas.com/parks/bracken.php

San Antonio: San Antonio Botanical Garden, www.sabot.org

Tyler: Tyler Municipal Rose Garden, www.cityoftyler.org

Victoria: Victoria Memorial Rose Garden, www.discoverourtown.com/TX/local-27834.html

Weatherford: Chandor Gardens, www.chandorgardens.com